BENTHAM:
A GUIDE FOR THE PERPLEXED

Continuum *Guides for the Perplexed*

Continuum's Guides for the Perplexed are clear, concise and accessible introductions to thinkers, writers and subjects that students and readers can find especially challenging. Concentrating specifically on what it is that makes the subject difficult to grasp, these books explain and explore key themes and ideas, guiding the reader towards a thorough understanding of demanding material.

Guides for the Perplexed **available from Continuum**
Adorno: A Guide for the Perplexed, Alex Thomson
Arendt: A Guide for the Perplexed, Karin Fry
Aristotle: A Guide for the Perplexed, John Vella
Berkeley: A Guide for the Perplexed, Talia Bettcher
Deleuze: A Guide for the Perplexed, Claire Colebrook
Derrida: A Guide for the Perplexed, Julian Wolfreys
Descartes: A Guide for the Perplexed, Justin Skirry
Existentialism: A Guide for the Perplexed, Stephen Earnshaw
Freud: A Guide for the Perplexed, Celine Surprenant
Gadamer: A Guide for the Perplexed, Chris Lawn
Habermas: A Guide for the Perplexed, Eduardo Mendieta
Hegel: A Guide for the Perplexed, David James
Heidegger: A Guide for the Perplexed, David Cerbone
Hobbes: A Guide for the Perplexed, Stephen J. Finn
Hume: A Guide for the Perplexed, Angela Coventry
Husserl: A Guide for the Perplexed, Matheson Russell
Kant: A Guide for the Perplexed, T. K. Seung
Kierkegaard: A Guide for the Perplexed, Clare Carlisle
Leibniz: A Guide for the Perplexed, Franklin Perkins
Levinas: A Guide for the Perplexed, B. C. Hutchens
Merleau-Ponty: A Guide for the Perplexed, Eric Matthews
Nietzsche: A Guide for the Perplexed, R. Kevin Hill
Plato: A Guide for the Perplexed, Gerald A. Press
Pragmatism: A Guide for the Perplexed, Robert B. Talisse and Scott F. Aikin
Quine: A Guide for the Perplexed, Gary Kemp
Relativism: A Guide for the Perplexed, Timothy Mosteller
Ricoeur: A Guide for the Perplexed, David Pellauer
Rousseau: A Guide for the Perplexed, Matthew Simpson
Sartre: A Guide for the Perplexed, Gary Cox
Spinoza: A Guide for the Perplexed, Charles Jarrett
The Stoics: A Guide for the Perplexed, M. Andrew Holowchak

BENTHAM:
A GUIDE FOR THE PERPLEXED

PHILIP SCHOFIELD

continuum

Continuum International Publishing Group

The Tower Building   80 Maiden Lane
11 York Road   Suite 704
London SE1 7NX   New York NY 10038

www.continuumbooks.com

© Philip Schofield 2009

All rights reserved. No part of this publication may be reproduced or
transmitted in any form or by any means, electronic or mechanical,
including photocopying, recording, or any information storage
or retrieval system, without prior permission
in writing from the publishers.

British Library Cataloguing-in-Publication Data
A catalogue record for this book is available from the British Library.

ISBN-10: HB: 0-8264-9589-3
          PB: 0-8264-9590-7
ISBN-13: HB: 978-0-8264-9589-1
          PB: 978-0-8264-9590-7

Library of Congress Cataloging-in-Publication Data
Schofield, Philip.
Bentham: a guide for the perplexed / Philip Schofield.
p. cm.
ISBN 978-0-8264-9589-1
ISBN 978-0-8264-9590-7
1. Bentham, Jeremy, 1748-1832. I. Title.
B1574.B34S36 2009
192–dc22

2008039191

Typeset by Newgen Imaging Systems Pvt Ltd, Chennai, India
Printed and bound in Great Britain by MPG Books Ltd,
Bodmin, Cornwall

CONTENTS

ACKNOWLEDGEMENTS

This is both a challenging and an exciting time for Bentham studies. The new authoritative edition of *The Collected Works of Jeremy Bentham*, which is being produced by the Bentham Project at University College London, is providing scholars with not only better versions of previously published texts, but also new and hitherto unknown texts. These texts are gradually emerging from the Bentham Papers deposited in UCL Library and the British Library. The result is that, until the edition is complete, all that is written about Bentham must, to some greater or lesser degree, be regarded as provisional. As the current General Editor of the new edition, I am all too aware that, due to the Project's research on the Bentham Papers, received views about Bentham's life and thought have often been shown to be inaccurate or in need of modification. The present book draws on some of the latest work being undertaken at the Bentham Project, but between sending this book to the press and its publication, there are sure to be new discoveries!

I am grateful to my colleagues at the Bentham Project – Catherine Fuller, Catherine Pease-Watkin, Irena Nicoll, Oliver Harris and Michael Quinn – for their help, advice, support and encouragement. I am especially grateful to Michael Quinn and Catherine Fuller for reading and commenting on several of the chapters in this book. I should add that a great deal of what is said in Chapter Four in relation to the poor laws draws on numerous conversations with Michael Quinn, as he attempted to explain to me just what it was that Bentham was trying to do with his 'census' of the pauper population. Thanks are also due to Kate Barber, the Project's administrator, who has supported my work in all sorts of ways. I am grateful to Gill Furlong and Susan Stead and their colleagues at UCL Library who look after the Bentham Papers. Finally, I would like to thank the worldwide community of Bentham scholars (a small but select group of right-minded persons!) who help to make the study of Bentham so stimulating, and (dare I say it) pleasurable.

In the 'Advertisement' to *A View of the Hard-Labour Bill*, published in 1778, Bentham noted: 'In regard to *sex*, I make, in general, no separate mention of the *female*; that being understood (unless where the contrary is specified) to be included under the expression used to denote the *male*.' I have followed Bentham's policy in the following pages. I hope that females everywhere – and especially my wife Kathryn and daughters Rebecca and Abigail – will be generous enough to forgive me.

I would like to dedicate this book to the students who have, over the years, endured my teaching on UCL's LLM and MA course on Jeremy Bentham and the Utilitarian Tradition.

Philip Schofield
UCL, August 2008

ABBREVIATIONS

BL Add. MS   British Library Additional Manuscript.

Bowring   Bentham, J. (1843), *The Works of Jeremy Bentham*. J. Bowring (ed.), 11 vols, Edinburgh: William Tait.

IPML   Bentham, J. (1970), *An Introduction to the Principles of Morals and Legislation*. J. H. Burns and H. L. A. Hart (eds), London: Athlone Press.

UC   University College London Library, Bentham Papers. (Roman numerals refer to the boxes in which the papers are placed, and Arabic to the folios within each box.)

CHAPTER ONE

WHO WAS JEREMY BENTHAM?

BIRTH, FAMILY AND EDUCATION

Jeremy Bentham was born in Houndsditch, London on 15 February 1748.[1] He was the eldest son of Alicia Whitehorn, née Grove, who on 3 October 1745 had entered into her second marriage with Jeremiah Bentham, a successful practitioner in the Court of Chancery, with wealthy and important clients in the City of London, but who seems to have made most of his money through property speculation.[2] Six further children were born, of whom only the youngest, Samuel, born in 1757, survived beyond infancy. Death was never far away, and on 6 January 1759, when Jeremy was 10 years old, he lost his mother. Jeremy himself was not expected to survive infancy, though by 1755 he was considered robust enough to go to Westminster School. His grandmothers were the most important influences in his early childhood, and he spent the school vacations at their houses in Barking, Essex and at Browning Hill in Baughurst, Hampshire. They were both daughters of clergymen, and raised their grandson to be a devout member of the Church of England. They taught him the Catechism, and he attended their daily prayers.[3] There was, however, another early influence, which may have given him a rather different perspective on life, and that was John Mulford, his mother's cousin. According to Bentham's later recollection, Mulford was 'a sort of rake', of an engaging, lively and practical disposition, who seems to have been very fond of young Jeremy. It may have been Mulford who encouraged Bentham's interest in botany, chemistry and medicine – interests he retained throughout life.[4] Bentham was, moreover, a voracious reader – despite his parents' view 'that books of amusement were unfit for children'[5] he managed to read Swift's *Gulliver's*

Travels, Defoe's *Robinson Crusoe* and Richardson's *Clarissa*, though Sterne's *Tristram Shandy* was snatched out of his hands by his father. He even profited from such demanding works as Locke's *Essay Concerning Human Understanding*, Clarendon's *History of the Civil Wars*, Milton's *Paradise Lost* and *Paradise Regained*, and, a particular favourite, Fénelon's *Telemachus*.[6] As would be expected of the son of an eighteenth-century gentleman, he studied, and quickly became proficient in, French, Latin and Greek.

Recognizing that his eldest child was a prodigy, Jeremiah sent him, at the tender age of 12, to Queen's College, Oxford, where he took up residence in October 1760. He was never happy at Oxford, and had to be moved from his first room which overlooked a graveyard on account of the nightmares it produced. His fear of ghosts, and associated nightmares, remained with him throughout his life. Even his graduation with a Bachelor of Arts degree in 1764 (he was reputedly the youngest person up to that time ever to graduate) proved extremely problematic. Graduation was conditional upon the graduand swearing to the statements of faith and discipline contained in the Thirty-nine Articles of the Church of England. Bentham could not bring himself to accept them. He realized, however, that not to swear, and thereby to disqualify himself from receiving his degree, would destroy his relationship with his father, who expected him to pursue a brilliant legal career, and even rise to the office of Lord Chancellor at the pinnacle of the profession. Bentham later recalled that by his 'ill-timed scruples, and the consequent public disgrace', his father's 'fondest hopes would have been blasted, the expenses he had bestowed on my education bestowed in vain'. On the other hand, to swear to the Articles was an act of intellectual dishonesty. In the event, he swore, but it was a decision he always regretted, as he made clear over 50 years later: 'by the view I found myself forced to take of the whole business, such an impression was made, as will never depart from me but with life.'[7] What is remarkable about this episode is that Bentham was a mere 16 years old at the time. His scepticism in relation to religious belief already ran deep, though the precise nature of that scepticism is not easy to discern. Many have concluded that Bentham must have been an atheist,[8] but there is no direct evidence for this view in that he refused, as a matter of principle, to express his personal religious views.[9] This episode also highlights the difficulties in Bentham's relationship with his father, which was complex, and often fraught with tension. There was friction over money, or rather the lack of it, so far as Jeremy was concerned; over Jeremiah's second marriage in 1766 to Sarah Abbot, née Farr, which brought two stepbrothers into the family, one of whom, Charles Abbot, later attained renown as Speaker of the House of Commons and was ennobled for his efforts; over Jeremy's desire, communicated to his father in April 1775, to marry Polly Dunkley, which Jeremiah strongly opposed on the grounds of her low social status (despite himself having married the daughter of a mercer); over Jeremy's career; and, of course, over religion. But, as Bentham famously remarked in *A Fragment on Government*, '[u]nder a government of Laws, . . . the motto of a good citizen' was *'[t]o obey punctually; to censure freely'*.[10] Under the government of his father, Bentham's motto was to obey punctually, and to keep his thoughts to himself.

In 1762 Jeremiah had moved his family to Queen's Square Place, Westminster, where he bought a comfortable house with an enormous garden, with its own entrance onto St James's Park, where Bentham would later in life take up jogging. In January 1763 Bentham had been admitted to Lincoln's Inn, and later that year began to eat the requisite number of dinners for eventual qualification as a barrister. He spent the next few years studying law, attending the great English law courts which sat in Westminster Hall. He returned to Oxford to hear the lectures of William Blackstone, the first Vinerian Professor of English law. The lectures would later in the decade be published as *Commentaries on the Laws of England*,[11] and immediately be recognized as the classic exposition of English law – and provide Bentham with a lifelong target.[12] In 1769 he was admitted to the bar. His main residence for many years – until 1792 when he inherited his father's home in Queen's Square Place – was his chambers in Lincoln's Inn. His attempt to practise law, however, was short-lived. When on one occasion he did receive a brief, he advised his client to give up the case on the grounds that the costs of pursuing his claim would outweigh any sum he could hope to recover.[13] This was not the behaviour of a typical lawyer.

The year 1769 – 'a most interesting year' as Bentham himself called it[14] – was important for a different reason. It was in 1769 that Bentham found a purpose for his life. All the pieces of the jigsaw suddenly came into place. His later reflections on this period of his life reveal an exposure to a very different literature from the one he had been allowed to peruse as a child. Prominent now were names such as Montesquieu, Helvétius, Beccaria and Voltaire – figures associated with the continental Enlightenment – and David Hume, David Hartley and Joseph Priestley – figures who were advancing radical philosophical and political views. Bentham brought together various elements from these thinkers to construct his version of the principle of utility. We will look in more detail at the principle of utility in Chapter Three,[15] but suffice it for now to say that he recognized that there existed a link between pleasure and pain on the one side, and happiness and suffering on the other; that the promotion of pleasure (happiness) and the diminution of pain (suffering) constituted the only proper basis for the standard of right and wrong; and that this standard, expressed by the phrase 'the greatest happiness of the greatest number', was the proper end of morals and legislation. And it was about the same time that he asked himself the question, 'Have I a *genius* for anything? What can *I* produce?' And then another question, 'What of all earthly pursuits is the most important?' The answer given by Helvétius to the second question was legislation. Hence, Bentham reformulated the question: 'have I indeed a genius for legislation?' He answered himself 'fearfully and tremblingly – Yes!'[16] An answer which would have immense consequences not only for Bentham, but for the subsequent course of philosophy, law and politics.

JURISPRUDENCE

Bentham spent the remaining six decades and more of his life writing on legislation, broadly conceived – in other words on law and legal procedure, punishment and reward, ethics, politics, economics and social policy, and religion. The first major task he set himself was to produce a complete penal code, to which his most famous work, *An Introduction to the Principles of Morals and Legislation* (printed in 1780 and published in 1789) was intended as a preface.[17] He had earlier published *A Fragment on Government* in 1776, an attack on Blackstone's *Commentaries on the Laws of England*, which, as noted above, was based on lectures given at the University of Oxford which Bentham had attended. Bentham needed to make a name for himself – he reckoned that, in order to marry Polly Dunkley, he needed to increase his income, and he could do this by publishing a devastating attack on the leading legal writer of his age. *A Fragment on Government* was, therefore, published anonymously, and gained some degree of attention. Jeremiah, now acting the role of the proud father, let it be known that his son was the author. But once it was discovered that the author was an obscure, briefless barrister, all interest in the work ceased; sales dried up; and Jeremy did not acquire a fortune sufficient to marry Polly.

The work is, nevertheless, a seminal text in the field of jurisprudence – the issues which Bentham raised still define and dominate debates in contemporary legal theory. Bentham offered three main criticisms of Blackstone. First, he criticized Blackstone's methodology, itself a product of his adoption of a mistaken moral theory – the theory of natural law. Blackstone had failed to distinguish between the role of the expositor, which was to describe the law as it existed in a particular legal system, and that of the censor, which was to explain what the law ought to be. Blackstone's confusion of the question of 'what the law is' with the question of 'what the law ought to be' had led him to assume that law as it existed in England was more or less perfect, and not in need of any significant reform. It is Bentham's clarification of the distinction between 'is' and 'ought' which eventually led to the emergence of the modern doctrine of legal positivism, which, in the classic form in which it is expressed by H. L. A. Hart, the twentieth century's most important legal philosopher and, incidentally, a noted scholar of Bentham, claims that law and morality are conceptually distinct.[18] Second, Bentham criticized Blackstone's support for the theory of the social contract as an adequate explanation of the foundation of government. Third, he criticized Blackstone's theory of sovereignty, which claimed that in every state there must exist some absolute, undivided power, whose commands were law. Bentham pointed out that there existed states where sovereign power was both divided and limited. *A Fragment on Government* was not, however, mere criticism. Bentham outlined a number of themes which would characterize his later works: the habit of obedience as the basis of government; the importance of a 'natural arrangement' for a legal system, whereby actions were placed in the category of offences in so far as they produced more pain than pleasure; the point at which resistance to government became justified; a proper method for the exposition of legal terms; and much more. Moreover, it is possible to interpret *A Fragment on Government* as a contribution to the major political issue of the day – American independence. Even though not explicitly directed to the American controversy, Bentham's attempt to tackle such issues as sovereignty and the right of resistance must have had resonance in that context. Add to this Bentham's collaboration with his friend John Lind on the latter's pamphlets in support of the British government against the claims of the colonists,[19] and a compelling case begins to emerge.[20]

In the late 1770s and early 1780s Bentham spent much of his time developing his notion of the science of legislation, founded upon the principle of utility. As noted above, one result of this endeavour was *An Introduction to the Principles of Morals and Legislation*. Here he argued that the right and proper end of government was the happiness of the community – a proposition which we will discuss in Chapter Three[21] – and went on to develop his theory of punishment, and produce a detailed classification of offences. In relation to punishment, he found inspiration in the work of Cesare Beccaria, who had stressed the importance of deterrence, proportionality and certainty of infliction.[22] Bentham took Beccaria's ideas, related them systematically to the principle of utility, and added elements of his own. He argued that the legislator, when assigning punishment to actions, had to take account of the 'profit' which accrued to the criminal, and the 'mischief' which resulted to the community, from the commission of the offence. This mischief consisted not merely in the 'primary' mischief of the loss suffered by the victim, but also in the 'secondary' mischief of the danger and alarm created in the community: danger represented the actual chance of harm, while alarm represented the fear of suffering harm, from criminal activity. I may, for instance, be in danger from the mad axeman who is standing outside my door, but because I am oblivious to his presence, I experience no alarm. On the other hand, I may experience alarm because of my fear of the mad axeman who murdered someone in my town a few days ago, but I am not in fact in any danger because, unbeknown to me, he has fled the country. The legislator had also to consider the amount of punishment which needed to be inflicted, the sort of punishment (Bentham favoured fines and imprisonment, because of their flexibility), and its certainty, that is the chance which the offender possessed of being caught, sentenced and punished accordingly. The point was to arrange affairs so that the potential offender calculated that he would be worse off if he committed the offence – in other words, he no longer had any motive to do so in that he calculated that the certainty and quantity of the punishment outweighed the expected 'profit'.[23]

As we have already seen, in *A Fragment on Government*, when discussing the natural arrangement of a legal system, Bentham had explained that any act which produced more pain than pleasure was potentially an offence. In *An Introduction to the Principles of Morals and Legislation* he produced a detailed classification of offences which began with an analysis of the persons who were affected by the offences in question. These persons could be grouped into four classes: one's self; a particular or assignable individual; a group of unassignable individuals, that is a group of persons who could not be individually identified; and the community at large. He then analysed each of these categories in turn. Just to give a flavour of his analysis, let us take the category of offences against individuals. Such offences could be divided into offences against the person, property, reputation or condition in life (status) of individuals (these four elements constituted an individual's security, as we shall see below); offences against the person in turn could be divided into offences against the mind and offences against the body; the latter in turn could be divided into corporal injuries, restraint or compulsion, confinement or banishment, and homicide.[24] An important consequence of this classification was that certain actions which had traditionally been punished – particularly those which concerned religious and sexual practices – would be found to produce no pain and should, therefore, not be subject to legal prohibition and penalty.[25]

As he worked on the text which became *An Introduction to the Principles of Morals and Legislation*, Bentham became aware that in order to produce a code of laws, he needed to understand what a single (or individuated) law consisted in. But he also realized that neither he, nor any one who had written before him, had properly defined what was meant by the notion of a law – just what was this entity which was termed a law? Bentham embarked on an investigation which produced the text hitherto known as *Of Laws in General* in which he argued, with incredible insight and sophistication, that a law was an expression of will on the part of a sovereign, who in turn was the person or body of persons, or some combination of persons and bodies, to whom the community was in a habit of obedience.[26] Around the same time, he came to the conclusion that the most effective means of promoting the happiness of the community would be through the introduction of a complete code of laws, or a 'pannomion' as he termed it.[27] Such a code would be 'all-comprehensive' and 'rationalized'. This meant that the code would be logically complete, in that all the terms used in the code would be clearly defined and anomalies and inconsistencies avoided, and that each single provision would be immediately followed by the reasons which justified it, such justification bearing reference of course to the principle of utility.[28]

At the apex of the pannomion would be the civil code, concerned with the distribution of rights and duties. The ultimate purpose of the civil law was to maximize the four sub-ends of utility, namely subsistence, abundance, security and equality.[29] The purpose of the penal law was to give effect to the civil law, by means of attaching punishment to those actions which, on account of their tendency to diminish happiness, had been classified as offences. Bentham was aware, however, that reward might perform the same function as punishment in attaching a sanction to an action, and thus give rise to a remuneratory code, but he thought that in practice such a code would probably be unnecessary and recognized that it would be too expensive. The constitutional code was, at least in part, also distributive in character, being concerned with the powers, rights and duties of public officials, and their modes of appointment and dismissal. As with the civil law, the penal law would give effect to the relevant parts of the constitutional law. The penal, civil and constitutional law together formed the substantive law, which was itself given effect by the adjective law, or the law of judicial procedure. The chain was completed by the law concerning the judicial establishment, whose purpose was to give effect to the adjective law, and thence to the substantive law. In other words, the civil code, and to some extent the constitutional code, would contain the 'directive rules' by which rights and duties were distributed, while the penal code would contain the sanctions 'by which provision is made for the observance of those directive rules'. To put this another way, the penal code would contain a statement of the sanctions attached to those actions which were classified as offences, while the civil code would contain an exposition of the terms which were made use of in the penal code. For instance, the penal code would forbid and sanction interference with property without title, while the civil code would explain 'what belongs to the several *sorts of titles*'. In terms of promulgation, the penal code would take priority, though the civil code, being closer to the 'common end', the promotion of happiness, was of greater importance.[30]

Bentham's commitment to codification was his solution to what he regarded as the profound failings of the English Common Law, a subject to which we will return in Chapter Seven.[31] His *desiderata* for a body of law, and which an all-comprehensive, rationalized code would achieve, were, '*[u]tility, notoriety, completeness, manifested reasonableness*'.[32] The Common Law, in contrast, was corrupt, unknowable, incomplete and arbitrary. It was so inadequate as a system of law that it could not perform the minimum purpose for which law was instituted, namely to guide conduct. Still less was it able to afford protection to those basic interests of the individual – his person, property, reputation and condition in life (what we would today refer to as status, such as the rights and duties of husbands and wives, of employers and employees, and so forth) – which constituted his security, and hence a major component of his well-being. Security was closely related to the notion of expectations, for it not only involved the present possession, but also the future expectation of possessing, the property you had lawfully acquired, present and future protection from physical harm, and so forth. Without security, and thus the confidence to project oneself and one's plans into the future, there could be no civilized life. Security was a product of law, resulting from the imposition of rules on conduct. In one respect, it did not matter which set of rules were imposed, so long as some set of rules were imposed, and these rules were known and certain, although the best rules were of course those sanctioned by the principle of utility. The crux of the problem with the Common Law was that those subject to it did not, and could not, know what it ordained, and this created uncertainty. Expectations could either not be formed or were constantly liable to be disappointed; and the consequence was insecurity.[33]

THE TRANSITION TO DEMOCRACY

Although Bentham had developed a detailed programme of legal reform by the early 1780s, he showed little sign of appreciating the political problems which might be involved in establishing his ideal system of law. The 'eighteenth-century Bentham' appeared willing to work with any political regime, believing that once the best course of legislation had been pointed out to them, rulers would adopt it. As he later reminisced to John Bowring, he 'never suspected that the people in power were against reform. I supposed they only wanted to know what was good in order to embrace it.'[34] However, by the 1820s, Bentham was convinced that the only regime with an interest in enacting good legislation was a representative democracy, and had, therefore, committed himself to political radicalism.[35] Scholars have disagreed over precisely when this change took place. The one thing which everyone agrees is that Bentham's writings on parliamentary reform, on which he commenced work in the summer of 1809, and in which he presents a utilitarian justification for 'democratic ascendancy' in the British political system, mark the commencement of the open avowal of his radicalism.

The standard view has been that Bentham was converted to political radicalism in 1808–9 when he came into contact with James Mill, the philosopher, economist, historian and arch-promoter of Bentham's ideas.[36] The problem with this hypothesis is that there is no evidence, beyond a coincidence of dates, that James Mill converted or transformed Bentham into a political democrat. It would be just as plausible to suggest that Bentham converted James Mill to political radicalism, or that it was a view which they arrived at together.

A second view is that of Mary Mack, who has argued that Bentham became a political radical in 1790 under the influence of the French Revolution. In the light of government suppression of radical activity in the early 1790s, he became politically quiescent for tactical reasons, and so, when he began to write on parliamentary reform in 1809, he simply picked up where he had left off 20 years earlier.[37] J. H. Burns, in contrast, has argued that Bentham's defence of democracy in France should not be extrapolated into a support for political radicalism more generally.[38] Following the publication of Bentham's writings on the French Revolution,[39] it is now clear that Mack's view is untenable. Bentham did in September 1789 recommend universal suffrage (including female suffrage) in a draft constitution which he produced for the French, but this did not represent anything more than a specific proposal aimed at the extraordinary circumstances then existing in France. As the French Revolution became more extreme, Bentham, like the overwhelming majority of his countrymen, began to fear for the stability of British society, particularly when threatened with the prospect of a French invasion.[40] In the 1790s Bentham pursued a strategy of promoting security – through his panopticon prison scheme, poor law proposals, and financial reform – in response to what he saw as the threat to social order emanating from France. This was not a 'tactical withdrawal' from radical politics, but a serious contribution to the attempt to maintain, and indeed extend, the benefits enjoyed under the British Constitution.[41]

A third view is that it was the rejection of the panopticon prison scheme which was the crucial factor. From about 1790 to 1803 Bentham's life was dominated by his attempt to build a panopticon prison in London. The panopticon, which will be discussed in more detail in Chapter Four,[42] was the brainchild of Bentham's brother Samuel, when employed in the 1780s on the estates of Prince Potemkin at Krichëv in the Crimea, part of the Russian Empire. He found that, by organizing his workforce in a circular building, with himself at the centre, he could supervise their activities more effectively. Visiting Samuel in the late 1780s and seeing the design, Bentham immediately appreciated its potential. Enshrining the principle of inspection, the panopticon might be adapted as a mental asylum, hospital, school, poor house, factory and, of course, prison. The prison building would be circular, with the cells, occupying several storeys one above the other, placed around the circumference. At the centre of the building would be the inspector's lodge, which would be so constructed that the inspector would always be capable of seeing into the cells, while the prisoners would be unable to see whether they were being watched. The activities of the prisoners would be transparent to the inspector; his actions, insofar as the prisoners were concerned, were hid behind a veil of secrecy. On the other hand, it was a cardinal feature of the design that the activities of the inspector and his officials should be laid open to the general scrutiny of the public, who would be encouraged to visit the prison. Having devoted many years of his life, large sums of his money and considerable energy, trying to persuade the British government to build a prison on the panopticon plan, and trying to find an appropriate site for it, and even having had an Act of Parliament passed to authorize the scheme, he was left bitter and despondent when the plan was effectively quashed in 1803.[43] The view that panopticon was instrumental in Bentham's transition to political radicalism becomes plausible when it is appreciated that, from a theoretical point of view, the crucial development was his 'discovery' of sinister interests, that is the fact that rulers did not desire to promote the greatest happiness of the community, but rather their own greatest happiness. There was no point in showing rulers how best to promote the happiness of their subjects if they had no interest in doing so, and the only rulers who had such an interest were the members of a representative assembly elected by a democratic suffrage. Bentham began to write systematically about sinister interests in early 1804 (although the phrase 'sinister interest' appears as early as 1798),[44] before he came into contact with Mill. It was the panopticon experience which began to convince him that nothing worthwhile could be achieved through the existing political structure in Britain, and by analogy through similar regimes elsewhere.

While Bentham never did finally abandon his promotion of panopticon, and while hopes of reviving the London scheme waxed and waned until 1813 and the subsequent award of the generous sum of £23,000 in compensation, it would never again dominate his life. In 1803 he returned to what he knew best, namely, criticism of the English legal system, and in particular its procedure and associated rules of evidence. In trying to explain why the law of evidence was so complex and contradictory, he began to see that it was not the result of a lack of intelligence, but rather the result of a determined and studied policy to make the legal process expensive and convoluted, in order to guarantee large profits for the lawyers whom the ordinary litigant would need to conduct him through the labyrinth. In other words, the legal system had been fashioned in order to serve the sinister interests of lawyers. At first Bentham confined his criticism to the legal profession, believing that they had duped the rest of the community. But he soon came to realize that the conspiracy went further than this, and included the whole of the ruling classes (the ruling few, as Bentham termed them), for a further consequence of the expense associated with legal procedure was the denial of legal protection to the majority of the people (the subject many). Sinister interest, then, characterized the whole of the establishment. Ironically, it was a speech of his stepbrother Charles Abbot, delivered in the House of Commons on 1 June 1809, which prompted Bentham to commence work on the writings which he eventually published in 1817 as *Plan of Parliamentary Reform*. In this work he called for universal manhood suffrage (subject to a literacy test), annual parliaments, equal electoral districts, payment of MPs and the secret ballot. In 1818 a series of resolutions based on Bentham's ideas were presented to the House of Commons by Sir Francis Burdett, but not a single member voted in favour of them.[45] Bentham then went a stage further and drew up a blueprint

for representative democracy which would have seen the abolition of the monarchy, the House of Lords and all artificial titles of
honour, and would have rendered government entirely open and,
he hoped, fully accountable. These proposals were developed in
astonishing detail in his magisterial *Constitutional Code*, the work
which dominated the final decade of his life. By his death in 1832,
he was a republican, admiring the government of the United States
of America above all others in existence.

'LEGISLATOR OF THE WORLD'

By 1780 Bentham had become convinced of the need to replace
existing law with a codified system based on the principle of utility. In the final two decades of his life, as he developed his radical
political ideas, codification once again became his central practical as well as theoretical concern. In 1811 he initiated a campaign
to persuade a political state – any political state – to invite him
to draw up a code of laws, hence his correspondence with figures
as diverse as James Madison, President of the United States of
America, and Alexander I, the Russian Emperor.[46] On 22 April 1822
Bentham finally received the invitation which he had been long-
ing for: the Portuguese Cortes had formally accepted his offer to
draw up for them civil, penal and constitutional codes.[47] He immediately began to compose *Constitutional Code*, but unfortunately,
long before even the first volume of this work had been printed in
1827, the liberal regime which had accepted Bentham's offer had
been swept away. Undeterred, Bentham devoted time and attention to Spain,[48] Tripoli, Greece,[49] and the emerging states of Latin
America,[50] as well as becoming fully involved in the attempts made
to reform and codify English law. In the 1820s Bentham enjoyed
an international reputation as the doyen of liberal legal philosophers and political reformers (Bentham, incidentally, invented
the word 'international').[51] To take one example, José del Valle,
the Guatemalan lawyer, economist and politician, made strenu-
ous efforts to collect all of Bentham's books. One of these books
is prominently displayed in Valle's portrait, in which he wears a
mourning ring which Bentham had left to him in his will. It was
Valle who called Bentham 'legislator of the world'.[52]

It should be noted that Bentham was known throughout Europe,
and particularly in Spain and South America, not through his

original writings in English, but rather in the versions or recensions of his works produced in elegant French by his Genevan translator and editor Étienne Dumont, and in Spanish translations either from Bentham's English, or more importantly from Dumont's French. Bentham seems to have met Dumont in 1788, through the Marquis of Lansdowne, who (when titled the Earl of Shelburne)[53] had come into contact with Bentham around 1780, and who formed a centre of union for a group of intellectually advanced writers and thinkers, including Samuel Romilly and Joseph Priestley. This coterie has been called the Bowood Circle, after Lansdowne's country house in Wiltshire where they reputedly met. Bentham only visited Bowood twice, albeit for several weeks each time, but spent much more time at Lansdowne's house in London, which may have been a more fruitful location for the exchange of ideas.[54] It is not clear that the individuals who are said to have formed the Bowood Circle would have regarded themselves as belonging to such a group (there is no evidence that Bentham did so). Nevertheless, the contacts which Lansdowne was able to provide proved extremely important for Bentham, and none more so than that with Dumont. Their friendship blossomed as Dumont took it upon himself to become Bentham's translator and interpreter.[55] The collaboration resulted in the publication of five recensions between 1802 and 1828. These were not literal translations of Bentham's writings, but lucid distillations of Bentham's central ideas. The first, and most important, was *Traités de législation civile et pénale*, published at Paris in 1802, which made Bentham's name 'generally known in Europe to men in public situation'.[56] One early admirer of *Traités de législation civile et pénale* was no less a figure than the French Emperor Napoleon Bonaparte, to whom it had been shown by his Foreign Minister Talleyrand. According to Bentham, Napoleon had declared it to be 'un ouvrage de génie'.[57] Copies of *Traités de législation civile et pénale* were sent to Spain soon after its publication,[58] and eventually translated into Spanish by Ramón de Salas as *Tratados de legislación civile y penale*, which appeared at Madrid in five volumes in 1821–2. Towards the end of Bentham's life, Dumont's Parisian publishers reckoned that a total of 50,000 copies of *Traités de législation civile et pénale* had been sold, and a further 40,000 copies of Spanish translations of this and the other recensions.[59]

This international recognition was in great part founded on the recensions of Bentham's works produced in French by Dumont.

Why, then, did Bentham's ideas, as presented to the world through Dumont, carry such appeal? The early nineteenth century was a great age of law reform, inspired by the Enlightenment and the French legal codes, responding to the need to reconstruct states and legal systems, both in Europe and America, following the upheavals of the Napoleonic Wars. The legislator would play the key role: he would be at the forefront of reform, sweeping away the irrational institutions and practices of the past, and putting in their place institutions and laws based upon utilitarian principles. To statesmen who wished to reform, or even revolutionize, the political and legal systems of the states to which they belonged, but who faced resistance from entrenched interests such as the privileged nobility and the church, the rational, secular, reforming programme offered by Bentham must have appeared refreshing indeed. Bentham was an extreme critic of the legal systems which he found in existence, but at the same time he was profoundly optimistic about what could be achieved by law. As he had announced in *An Introduction to the Principles of Morals and Legislation*, his enterprise was 'to rear the fabric of felicity by the hands of reason and of law'.[60] However, it was the politically quiescent, enlightenment-inspired Bentham of the late 1770s and 1780s who was represented in Dumont's recensions, and not the radical, democratic, republican Bentham of the 1820s. Bentham was not overtly anti-religious in the Dumont-edited texts (Dumont himself seems to have been careful not to present Bentham in a way which betrayed too forthrightly his anti-religious sentiments), yet religion was, to anyone who considered the matter, not a necessary basis of his science of legislation (although one might read into Bentham's frequent appeals to 'nature' some sort of background divine presence, if one were inclined to do so). His vision of the law as an instrument of reform and improvement had great appeal in an age when a combination of ignorance, prejudice and superstition appeared to be the main barrier to human progress. He offered a secular vision of society, where the standard of rectitude would be founded not on theology, or natural law, or right reason, or precedent, or sheer prejudice, but on observation and analysis of experienced facts. Knowledge of society (and of the individuals who composed it) enshrined in a 'political science' would be the basis for the art of legislation, the practical measures which the utilitarian legislator would introduce in order to promote the greatest happiness of the community. Hence Bentham liked to think of himself as 'the Newton of legislation' – just as Newton had brought order, and thus understanding, to the physical sciences, so would Bentham to the moral sciences.[61]

BENTHAM'S ACHIEVEMENTS AND SIGNIFICANCE

What claims might plausibly be made about Bentham's achievements and his contemporary significance?[62] In ethics, Bentham was the founder of the modern doctrine of utilitarianism, which has been one of the most influential moral theories of the past 200 years and, within liberalism, remains the main rival to theories of human rights. Bentham's so-called felicific calculus[63] is the inspiration for cost–benefit analysis which dominates the contemporary discipline of economics.[64] In jurisprudence, the modern doctrine of legal positivism derives from Bentham's clarification of the distinction between 'law as it is' and 'law as it ought to be'.[65] In 'Nonsense upon Stilts' (until recently known under the title 'Anarchical Fallacies'), he launched the most devastating attack ever written on the doctrine of natural rights, the forerunner of modern conceptions of human rights.[66] In his extensive and detailed writings on judicial procedure, he produced the most comprehensive theory of evidence in the Anglo-American tradition.[67] He developed a systematic theory of punishment which emphasized deterrence, proportionality and the reformation of the offender,[68] which was complemented by a theory of reward – particularly in relation to official pay and the encouragement of economic activity – which was not even a subject of study before he wrote.[69] In politics, he produced, in 1789, the earliest utilitarian defence of political equality (advocating women's suffrage before the publication of Mary Wollstonecraft's *A Vindication of the Rights of Women*),[70] and later, in *Constitutional Code*, produced a sophisticated and detailed blueprint for representative democracy within a republican state.[71] His work on *Political Tactics* was the first systematic treatise on the organization of a political assembly.[72] The panopticon prison scheme, given a central place in Michel Foucault's interpretation of the nature of the modern state,[73] locates Bentham at the heart of debates about what it means to be modern (and post-modern).[74] The history of surveillance, on this view, begins with panopticon. According to Foucault, 'Bentham is more important for our society than Kant and Hegel.'[75] Bentham put forward a scheme to promote peace between nations, advocating an international court of arbitration and a proportional reduction of armed forces.[76] He argued that the European powers should emancipate their colonies – it was better for both mother country and colonies that the latter should govern themselves.[77] His writings on political economy were an important contribution to the development of classical political economy;[78] he was the first theorist of bureaucracy;[79] he had an enormous influence on legal and administrative reform more generally in nineteenth-century Britain;[80] in particular, his ideas on the administration of the poor laws inspired the Poor Law Amendment Act of 1834.[81] His educational ideas, based on 'useful learning' and access to all regardless of religion or gender (an intriguing title to one of his manuscripts reads 'Degrees, as in Universities – their uselessness', but he was talking about Oxford and Cambridge, where students had to be Anglican and male, and tended to study, if they studied at all, theology and dead languages),[82] was the inspiration for the establishment of the University of London (in 1836 renamed University College, London when it was united into a federal structure with the Church of England's King's College – not something that the Council of the University would have dared do, I fancy, if Bentham had still been alive).[83]

There immediately arises at least one perplexing question: how could a man, brought up in a highly conservative and devout family, with the prospect of a substantial inheritance and a social status that would gain him entry into almost any company, educated at a school and a university which we would today call pillars of the establishment, destined by his father for a career in a profession which was not noted for its love of innovation – how could a man from this background become such an original, if not revolutionary, thinker, and remain so in many respects nearly 200 years after his death? The place to start to answer this question is in a sort of 'self-assessment' contained in an essay titled 'J.B.'s new ideas derived from Logic', which Bentham composed in October 1814. At the head of his (apparently unfinished) list of 14 items is 'Division of entities into real and fictitious: or say, Division of nouns substantive into names of real entities and names of fictitious entities.' This distinction, which, he claimed, illuminated 'the whole field of logic, and thereby . . . the whole field of art and science',[84] was, perhaps, as original an idea as any philosopher has ever produced. By committing himself to this distinction as the basis of his philosophy, he was able to cast off all prepossessions, and genuinely to think about the world from first principles. The distinction will be explained in more detail in Chapter Three,[85] but what it amounts to is the claim that our language, and thereby our thought, only makes sense insofar as it is rooted in the physical world. Insofar as it is not rooted in the physical world, it is nonsense. The consequence of this is to dismiss all metaphysics as nonsense, and to place knowledge on the basis of experience and observation. This locates Bentham within the empirical tradition which had been inspired by Locke's *Essay Concerning Human Understanding*, but the tools of linguistic analysis developed by Bentham, which emerged from his distinction between real and fictitious entities, were more sophisticated than anything that Locke had managed to produce.

There are fascinating tensions in Bentham's thought: between Bentham as an 'authoritarian', where he seems to suggest that the ruler knows what is best for his subjects, and Bentham as a 'liberal', where he states that each individual is the best judge of what it is that gives him pleasure; between Bentham's recognition of what ideally is required by the principle of utility, and what in the circumstances in question is practicable – a recognition, as he put it, 'of the influence of time and place on matters of legislation'[86] – operating on a human nature which is universal in its desire for pleasure and aversion to pain. There is also dynamism in Bentham's thought. He developed and changed his ideas in response to the changing world about him – he was born at the end of the Augustan Age, came to maturity under the influence of the Enlightenment, and died at the height of Romanticism; he lived through the American and French Revolutions; he was affected by the Napoleonic Wars and their aftermath; and he saw the transformations brought about by the Industrial Revolution. He also responded to new ideas: for instance, the novel arrangement of his workforce by brother Samuel led him to develop his panopticon schemes; the publication in 1798 of Robert Malthus's *An Essay on the Principle of Population* had a deep impact on his social and economic thought; and the functioning of democracy in the United States of America inspired his own commitment to republican government. But what is perhaps most impressive about Bentham, and it was highlighted in his response to the requirement to subscribe to the Thirty-nine Articles, was his intellectual honesty – he was never afraid to follow his ideas to what he regarded as their logical conclusion. In this, he is an inspiration to all who value the unimpeded pursuit of knowledge.

CHAPTER TWO

WHICH BENTHAM?

WHO READS WHAT?

In a number of related disciplines, such as philosophy, political theory, jurisprudence, history of political thought and history of economic thought, we often refer collectively to those texts which form the staple of university undergraduate courses (e.g. Plato's *Republic*, Aristotle's *Politics* and Hobbes's *Leviathan*) as the 'canon'. We sometimes use the term in a more extended sense to refer to the larger group of such works which are read by more advanced researchers. In either case, the 'canon' is made up of 'texts'. The question of how one should study texts has greatly perplexed philosophers, even laying aside the question of how to choose what text or texts should be read. One prominent view is that the text should be read in order to extricate the truths, or more modestly the philosophical insights, which it might contain. A second prominent view is that we need to understand the intentions of the author if we are to grasp his meaning. And a third prominent view is that a text must be understood within its historical situation – the context – in which it was written, and this requires a historical study, among other things, of the circumstances which prompted the production of the work, of the influences on the author, of the texts to which he was responding, and of the conventions of the genre in which he was working.[1] What all these approaches assume is the existence of a text or a series of texts. Yet there is an even more fundamental issue than that concerning how one reads a text – namely, how is a text established or created in the first place? I am not here adopting the approach of the post-modern sceptic, who thinks that nothing that has ever been written, or ever will be written, has any inherent meaning, and that the only meaning it can have is whatever each of us chooses to project upon it; rather my perspective is that of a textual editor – a historian of political thought who has found himself editing the works of a major philosopher. In relation to the Bentham 'canon', the aggregate of texts that have been attributed to Bentham has changed radically in the past, is changing now, and will certainly change in the future. The point is that as new texts become available and as already-available texts are re-edited, the list of texts which constitute the Bentham canon undergoes significant change. Rather than being able to regard the canon as a rock on which we can stand with confidence, it appears to be more like sand which constantly shifts beneath our feet.

The standard source for the study of Bentham has been, and to a significant extent still is, the edition of his writings produced 'under the superintendence of' his literary editor John Bowring, and published in 11 volumes between 1838 and 1843. The Bowring edition contains most of the texts which Bentham himself published during his lifetime (though it excludes Bentham's published writings on religion);[2] texts which were edited by various 'disciples' of Bentham during his lifetime, including English translations of Dumont's recensions; and texts which were produced from Bentham's unpublished manuscripts after his death specifically for inclusion in the Bowring edition. Most subsequent reprints of Bentham's writings are derived either from the original works published by Bentham or from the Bowring edition. However, not only is the Bowring edition far from comprehensive, it does not seem to have been very widely read, and even where it has been read, it has been read very selectively. The Bentham 'canon' narrowly defined, therefore, can probably be restricted to one, two or possibly three works: the most popular is *An Introduction to the Principles of Morals and Legislation*, which, as noted in Chapter One,[3] was printed by Bentham in 1780, and published in 1789, with a slightly expanded second edition in 1823; then comes *A Fragment on Government*, Bentham's first major published work which appeared in 1776; and finally the so-called 'Anarchical Fallacies', written in 1795, but never published by Bentham himself, and which I will discuss below. Having said that, if one were to ask what constituted the Bentham 'canon' in the early nineteenth century, and particularly in the non-English speaking world, the answer would be Dumont's edition of *Traités de législation civile et pénale*, first published at Paris in 1802. It was this work which established

Bentham's reputation in places as far afield as Buenos Aries and St Petersburg (as we have seen in Chapter One,[4] it was retranslated into Spanish, but also into Russian, German and several other languages). As we have also seen in Chapter One,[5] Dumont went on to produce four more major recensions of Bentham's work, yet these works were not straightforward translations of Bentham's writings, but rather distillations of his key ideas, arranged in a way in which Dumont thought would appeal to the intended audience, and not necessarily in the way in which Bentham intended them to appear. I have already, therefore, identified three 'Benthams'. First, we have the Bentham who was known throughout Europe and America in the nineteenth century through the recensions of Dumont; second, we have the Bentham who is known to undergraduate students in philosophy or other related disciplines from the first few chapters of *An Introduction to the Principles of Morals and Legislation*; and third, we have the Bentham known to the more specialized scholar who is familiar with the Bowring edition (which at least has the virtue of a fairly detailed index).

But there is now a fourth Bentham, namely the Bentham who is beginning to emerge from the new authoritative edition of *The Collected Works of Jeremy Bentham*, being produced by the Bentham Project, based at University College London. The new *Collected Works* will, of coursc, supersede all previous versions of Bentham's writings, and especially the Bowring edition. As early as the 1930s it was recognized that the Bowring edition was poorly edited. In 1932 University College, London (it had a comma in its title until the 1980s), which had possession of around 60,000 folios of Bentham's manuscripts, decided to establish a Bentham Manuscripts Committee in order to oversee the publication of a new edition. Some half-hearted progress was made towards producing a volume of Bentham's economic writings, but even that modest enterprise was interrupted by the outbreak of the Second World War. It was not until the late 1950s, and prompted by the distinguished philosopher A. J. Ayer, that the authorities of University College, London once again gave serious consideration to the production of an authoritative edition. In 1959 the College established the Bentham Committee as a National Committee, under the chairmanship first of Lord Cohen, the judge, and then of Lionel Robbins, the economist, in order to oversee the production of the edition. J. H. Burns was appointed as the first General Editor in

1961, the scholars and researchers who worked on the edition came to be known collectively as the Bentham Project, and the first two volumes, which contained Bentham's correspondence up to the end of 1780, appeared in 1968. The present author is the fourth General Editor of the edition.

Why this is perplexing – and this can be extended to any other major philosopher – is that what we consider to be the Bentham canon, and from there what we consider to be Bentham's thought, ideas or world-view, will depend on just who it is that is doing the reading, in that they will be reading different things. If it is an early nineteenth-century South American politician, then the Bentham canon may be a Spanish translation of Dumont; if it is a contemporary undergraduate taking a course in the history of philosophy, then it may be the first six chapters of *An Introduction to the Principles of Morals and Legislation*; if it is an academic with a wide-ranging interest in the history of philosophy, it may be five or six texts which, he believes, contain the essence of Bentham's thought; and if it is the specialist scholar who has spent most of his career reading and writing about Bentham, then it is absolutely everything Bentham produced (such is my sad predicament). So, today, the Bentham canon may be said to consist in the first few pages of *An Introduction to the Principles of Morals and Legislation*, or it may consist in the texts typically discussed in the mainstream scholarly literature, or it may consist in all of the available texts, including unpublished manuscripts. There is no doubt that the new edition of Bentham's *Collected Works* has led to increased awareness of and thence interest in Bentham's thought, and has stimulated much excellent original scholarship, as hitherto unknown works have been published for the first time, or else rescued from the double-columned small print of the Bowring edition. And what seems beyond dispute is that as more texts become available, there are increased possibilities for a more nuanced and detailed understanding of Bentham's thought, and of its development over time. We can, therefore, construct a much more accurate account of Bentham's thought than the early nineteenth-century South American politician, but that does not alter the fact that, from a historian's point of view, the way in which Bentham was received in early nineteenth-century South America was through the texts which were available there and then, and that must never be lost sight of when trying to assess any historical influence which Bentham may have had.

A further complication is that scholars from different disciplines have different purposes when they read texts. Take the distinction between a historical and a philosophical approach – that is, the distinction between a historian who wishes to produce an intellectual biography of Bentham, and a philosopher who wishes to produce a reconstruction of his 'system'.[6] These are two different enterprises: the former is an attempt to recover what David Lieberman terms the 'authenticity Bentham', namely, the Bentham who is emerging from the *Collected Works*, as opposed to the 'historical' Bentham, that is, Bentham as he was known to his audience in the past.[7] The latter enterprise is an attempt to present Bentham's thought in its most satisfactory form. The philosophical approach has produced some excellent Bentham scholarship in recent years, and has led to reconstructions of Bentham's utilitarianism that, according to the lights of contemporary political and moral philosophy, are either more coherent, more consistent, or more plausible than a historical reading of the texts would allow.[8] However, there is a tendency to attribute to the 'authenticity Bentham' views he did not hold, and could not have held. The philosophical reconstructions in question do, of course, take seriously the constraints imposed by a historical reading of Bentham's texts, but only up to a point. It is incumbent on the philosopher to be completely open about when that point has been reached.

The distinction between the historical and philosophical approaches may be illustrated by reference to A. J. Ayer's seminal essay on Bentham's principle of utility.[9] Ayer reconstructs Bentham's system in such a way that it is no longer vulnerable to certain standard philosophical criticisms, yet at the same time attributes this reconstruction to the 'historical Bentham'. The problem which Ayer addresses is how to reconcile Bentham's psychological theory with his ethics. As we shall see in more detail in Chapter Three,[10] Bentham argues that while each individual wishes to promote his own greatest happiness, what he ought to do is to promote the greatest happiness of the community as a whole. How, then, does Bentham expect the individual in fact to do what he ought to do – in other words, how does he expect to reconcile the interests of the individual with that of the community? Ayer suggests that Bentham attempts to do this not only by making 'the rewards of benevolence [i.e. promoting the greatest happiness of the community] . . . appear as attractive as possible' to the individual, but also 'in a very much more subtle way', even though Bentham did not himself 'appear to be aware' he was doing it. This 'very much more subtle way' consisted in appealing to people's emotions, and thereby exhorting or persuading them to do what the moral standard – the principle of utility – stipulated was right.[11] Ayer does not concern himself with whether this strategy was what the 'authenticity Bentham' actually had in mind, but it is a strategy which Ayer attributes to Bentham, 'whether he was aware of it or not'. In the course of his discussion Ayer reconstructs Bentham's doctrine in a further significant way, yet writes as if his reconstruction is attributable to the 'authenticity Bentham'. While Bentham understood the promotion of the happiness of the community in terms of maximizing the pleasure experienced by the members of that community, Ayer argues that what he really meant to maximize was preference satisfaction – in other words, the satisfaction of as many of each person's wishes or desires as possible.

As contemporary students of Bentham, we are struggling to come to terms with the shifting sand which the new edition represents. Yet, as that edition progresses, we should find an increasing amount of firm ground to cling to. Having said that, even when a text has been produced in a so-called authoritative edition, the extent to which it is 'authoritative' may be a matter of dispute. This leads us into the question of how does one produce an 'authoritative' text?

THE COLLECTED WORKS OF JEREMY BENTHAM

How, then, does the Bentham Project go about its task of editing Bentham texts? We have already discussed the difference between a historical and a philosophical approach to reading a text. If one translates the historical and philosophical approaches into an editorial method for constructing a text, a very different text is likely to emerge. The historian will aim to produce the text as Bentham intended it (taking into account the fact that Bentham's intentions may have changed in the course of writing), whereas the philosopher will aim to produce a text which, by his lights, puts the argument in the most convincing or most coherent way. What is important to note is that a historical approach to editing, where author's intentions take priority, is not incompatible with the philosophical enterprise; but that a philosophical approach, where presenting a coherent system of thought takes priority, undermines, and perhaps makes impossible, the historical enterprise. Perhaps this is why most textual editors are historians, and philosophers have the good sense to allow them to get on with the job.

The approach of the Bentham Project is to construct the text in a way which is faithful to Bentham's intentions. We have already seen that a different methodology would produce a very different text. Yet it is also true that a different editor using the same methodology might also produce a very different text. For instance, the first volume that I edited for the *Collected Works* is titled *First Principles preparatory to Constitutional Code*, and appeared in 1989. This volume is based entirely on original manuscripts, most of which were written in 1822, and many of which were previously unpublished. The material it contains is now fairly well known by those Bentham scholars who have an interest in his democratic political theory. To those scholars it has become part of the canon. Yet it is quite possible that had some other person started from the point at which I started in editing that volume, he would have produced a volume which would have differed, and differed in a significant number of respects – for instance, in terms of the essays it contained; in terms of the structure of those essays; in terms of the detailed transcription of the manuscripts; in terms of the accompanying annotation; and even in terms of the title of the volume. The best that the editor can do is to be as explicit as possible in the editorial introduction to the volume in explaining how he has constructed the text in question.

A number of factors, both scholarly and non-scholarly, affect the production of the new Bentham edition. At the outset it was decided by the Bentham Committee that the edition should be 'comprehensive in scope as well as definitive in text'. This statement appears in the 'General Preface' to the edition which appeared in *Correspondence: Vol. I* (the first volume to be published in 1968). The 'General Preface' sets out the rationale for the edition, and lays down its proposed structure (i.e. the subject categories, such as 'Principles of Legislation', 'Economics and Society' and 'Constitutional Law', into which it was intended that the edition be divided).[12] That the edition should be 'comprehensive' remains the policy of the Bentham Committee – though we are now more cautious about the claim that the edition will be 'definitive', and prefer to say 'authoritative'. The subject categories as originally conceived have been retained. However, as knowledge about Bentham's surviving manuscripts has increased, the original estimate that the edition would run to 38 volumes has been revised upwards to the present estimate of 68 volumes.

It should be pointed out that in practice the edition is divided into two areas: the correspondence and the works. The correspondence aims to be both 'comprehensive' and 'complete', including all known letters written by and written to Bentham. To date, 12 of 14 projected volumes of correspondence have appeared, containing Bentham's letters through to the end of June 1828. The remaining 54 projected volumes belong to the works. Of these, 14 have been published, and the 15th – the second and final volume of *Writings on the Poor Laws* – is due for publication in 2009. Many of the published volumes deal with Bentham's political and constitutional thought, though individual volumes deal with ethics, education and codification.[13] At the moment, a significant amount of work is being done on Bentham's legal writings, in particular in the areas of judicial procedure and evidence. Other volumes dealing with logic and language and with political fallacies are also being prepared for publication. There are, however, large areas of Bentham's writings which are still to be explored. In the general area of Bentham's legal writings, little work has been done on the panopticon prison, on the civil, penal and procedural codes, on real property, and on law reform. Elsewhere, serious work is only just beginning on the economic writings and on the religious writings, on the early writings on jurisprudence, and on the theory of reward and punishment. The point is that we still have only a partial canon of Bentham's works to study: Dumont's recensions were not 'pure' Bentham in the first place; the Bowring edition is incomplete and poorly edited; and the new authoritative edition is only a third of the way through its publishing programme.

And what about the volumes which have been published in the new edition? I have already intimated that they do not constitute a representative sample of Bentham's works (whatever that might look like). What criteria, then, are used in judging which volumes to prepare for publication now, and which to leave until some future time? Had ideal circumstances prevailed at the inception of the edition (and by ideal circumstances I mean the existence of guaranteed funding for the whole of the enterprise), it is unlikely that the volumes would have been published in the order in which they have actually been published. In such ideal circumstances, chronology would (or should) have determined the order of publication – in other words, Bentham's works would have been published in the order in which they were written, except where, for thematic reasons, a special argument could be made for grouping together works produced at different times. An alternative approach might have been to publish, in the first instance, those works which were considered to be the most important. But such an approach would run into the insuperable problem of deciding which volumes were in fact the most important. If each scholar with an interest in Bentham were asked to provide a list of the 26 volumes which should be published first, there would be as many different lists as there were scholars. Alas! some people seem to think that a single Bentham volume is one too many! Others lament the fact that Bentham destroyed the manuscripts for the works which he himself published, and would be delighted to have parallel editions of printed and manuscript text. To sum up – on the one hand no one would probably think that the volumes published to date are the most important, and on the other hand no one would agree which volumes are the most important. Indeed, such an assessment would only begin to be feasible *after* all the volumes had been edited and published.

Why, then, do we have the 26 that we do? Giving a high priority to publishing the correspondence makes sense in that, once identified, the material is on the whole relatively straightforward to organize, and casts considerable light on the works and projects with which Bentham was engaged at the time. Having said that, the works often cast light on the correspondence, and, to emphasize the point I made earlier, greatest benefit would have accrued had chronologically related correspondence and works volumes progressed hand in hand. Nevertheless, the correspondence can be viewed as the backbone of the edition, and given the apparently haphazard way in which the works are being published, the benefits to the editor of the works of having the relevant correspondence volumes published is immense. The question might then be revised to ask – why do we have the 14 works volumes which we do? The short answer is this: the Bentham Project has managed to raise funds to edit them.

The issue of fund-raising is central. The work on the Bentham edition is carried out by researchers who need to be paid a salary; they need offices in which to work; and they need access to books and libraries. All this costs money. I do not think it unfair to say that the British academic community has not solved the problem of how to fund long-term research projects in the humanities such as the Bentham Project, and is in some respects further away from a solution now than it has ever been. The way in which the Bentham Project is currently supported is problematic for all sorts of reasons. One is that it is impossible to provide secure employment for research staff. Another is that a significant proportion of the time of the General Editor of the edition is spent attempting to raise funds and to write reports, instead of editing Bentham. But most importantly, the way in which the current provision of funding operates is not conducive to organizing the staff of the Bentham Project in the way which would be most effective. Returning to my ideal world, I would not choose to organize the Bentham Project according to what I call a 'volume-centred structure', which is the way we are pretty well forced to organize it at present, but according to what I call a 'task-centred structure'.

When applying for funds, I try to match the declared interests and scope of a particular funding body both with a particular work or set of works of Bentham and with a researcher capable of editing the material. One approach is to find a person who is a specialist in a particular field and to appoint him to edit Bentham's writings in that field, for instance, a philosopher to edit Bentham's writings on logic and language. This approach, which has been favoured at various points in the history of the Bentham edition, has not proved to be a particularly happy one. What the Bentham Project needs is Bentham editors: that is not specialists in a particular academic discipline, and not even specialists in Bentham studies, but quite simply Bentham editors. Bentham editors are *sui generis*. The only sensible approach is, therefore, to *create* Bentham editors through training within the Bentham Project. Editing Bentham requires a combination of highly specialized skills. No one who joins the Bentham Project is a ready-formed Bentham editor. It takes years to train staff to become Bentham editors. Some staff leave the Project for other academic posts, others because their funding has expired, before attaining the necessary expertise to become an editor. Many academics would simply be incapable of becoming a Bentham editor, not because of any lack of intelligence, knowledge or commitment, but because very few people can combine a meticulous and methodical approach with the creativity which is needed when dealing with problems of textual construction and production of annotation (and I've not even mentioned the ability to read Bentham's handwriting!). One of the Project's researchers once said that she enjoyed reading telephone directories – this captures a sense of one of the qualities which is required. The challenge is to find the funds to keep these highly trained and specialist members of staff, who must, as things stand, be employed on a succession of relatively short-term contracts.

It is this very fund-raising process which makes the editorial task even more difficult than it might be, since it leads to the volume-centred structure which I mentioned above. Under our current volume-centred structure, a particular individual is assigned to the editing of a particular volume or set of volumes, and so given responsibility for taking that volume all the way through the editorial process from manuscript to publication. However, the tasks involved in this process are numerous and diverse, and include identification of the relevant material, transcription of the manuscripts, organization of manuscripts and establishment of the text, detailed editing of the text, research and writing of annotation, writing of the editorial introduction, production of collations, compiling of name and subject indexes, and proof-reading. It seems to me that it would make more sense for individuals to specialize in two or three of these areas, rather than to expect each individual to be an expert in all. For instance, one individual might have greater aptitude for transcription and textual editing, while another might have greater aptitude for researching and writing the annotation. Instead of a particular individual taking responsibility for each and every one of these editorial tasks on a particular volume, the volume would move through the hands of several individuals, each of whom would be an expert in one or two tasks. Hence, one person might identify the relevant manuscripts and transcribe them, another might establish the text, and a third might produce the annotation. The General Editor would continue to take an active supervisory and coordinating role in relation to each volume. In short, instead of an individual taking a single volume up through all these levels (the volume-centred structure), he would operate at one or two of these levels, and each volume would pass through his hands as it progressed towards publication (the task-centred structure).

The implementation of a task-centred structure would require a different funding regime. Instead of funds being given for the editing of a particular volume, the Project would require a steady source

of income which could be used to support a number of permanent, long-term staff who would take responsibility for specific tasks.
This would be more efficient in terms of the overall cost and time
of producing the edition, and might even lead to a better edition
in that individuals would be assigned to those tasks for which they
had displayed the greatest talent and in which they could develop
their expertise. But, as I say, funding bodies can be persuaded to
give grants to support a particular researcher (named or not named
in the application) in order to produce a volume. General grants,
which could be used to institute a task-centred approach, do not
exist. Under this latter approach, the Project would have to justify
the way it had spent money already received, as the basis for con-
tinuing funding, rather than explain how it intended to spend money
in the future should it receive any. Scholarly projects of long term,
national importance would then have secure funding – of course, if
the pot of available money was not increased, then other individual
scholars with their own pet projects would lose out. It is a question
of priorities.

INVENTING THE TEXT

Having discussed some of the issues pertinent to the scope of the
edition as a whole, I come now to some of the issues pertinent to
the scope of a particular volume in the edition. The place to begin
is with Bentham's manuscripts, most of which are deposited in
the Bentham Papers in University College London Library, but
of which a further significant collection is in the British Library.
When Bentham wrote, he invariably did so with a particular work
or project in mind – whether it was a brief letter on a topical issue
intended for a newspaper or a complete code of laws intended to
govern an empire. Hence, each folio will typically have a heading
which identifies the work or project to which it belongs. We know,
for instance, from the headings on the manuscripts, that there are
about 4,000 folios in the Bentham Papers on the topic of parliamentary reform. A more detailed investigation of this material reveals
that Bentham, over a period of about 10 years from 1809, wrote
a series of distinct works related to the more general topic, some
of which went through several drafts. This might be contrasted
with the manuscripts for Bentham's famous essay 'Nonsense upon
Stilts' (also known as 'Anarchical Fallacies'), which was written as

a single draft, probably in the space of 5 or 6 weeks, and for which there are around 300 folios. Editing this latter material is a much more straightforward task than editing the former.

In order to understand how we go about editing a text from manuscript, it is important to understand Bentham's working methods, and the sort of materials he generated, and their purposes. I will now give a brief description of the main categories of manuscript.

(a) *Text sheets.* A text sheet contains prose material in Bentham's hand. When Bentham had written a sequence of text, he would often correct it. Many of the text sheets, therefore, contain numerous additions (usually interlinear, but sometimes marginal), deletions and emendations. It is worth reiterating that when Bentham himself printed or published a particular text, he usually destroyed the manuscript material on which it was based. This means that most of the surviving text material relates to works which Bentham himself did not publish, or was written for a particular work but was then excluded from the printed version, or was written after the printed version appeared. The earlier text sheets often consist of double sheets of foolscap, with both sides of each sheet being commonly used. The later text sheets usually consist of single sheets of foolscap, with one side being commonly used. The sheets are ruled with a wide margin, in which Bentham inserted summaries, and with a double line at the top where he inserted the heading, and from about 1800 the date. Bentham usually added subheadings to the margin, and page numbers or several sequences of page numbers at the top of the manuscript.

(b) *Copy sheets* and *fair copy sheets.* If Bentham decided that the material he had written might be used for publication, or for private circulation, he would have the text copied by an amanuensis. He would often revise the copy, which may itself contain considerable additions, deletions and emendations. He might then order a fair copy to be made of this revised copy, and it would be this copy, perhaps once again corrected, which would be sent to the printer.

(c) *Marginal summary sheets.* Bentham's habit was to write summaries of the content of the text sheets in the margin. These marginal summaries were written in the form of short paragraphs and numbered consecutively. They were often copied out by an amanuensis onto separate sheets, which we term marginal summary sheets. The marginal summary sheets also bear occasional additions and emendations in Bentham's hand, and sometimes rudiments and plans. The marginal summary sheets are written on single sheets of foolscap ruled into four columns with a double line at the top for the date and the heading. The marginal summary sheets were not intended for publication, but rather were used by Bentham for purposes of reference. They form a very valuable tool for the ordering of Bentham's texts: a sequence of four or five marginal summary sheets, for instance, may correspond to twenty or thirty text sheets, whose ordering might not otherwise be obvious. In short, the marginal summary sheets are particularly valuable for reconstructing sequences of text where, for whatever reason, the text sheets have become disordered.

(d) *Rudiments sheets.* These are typically double sheets of foolscap ruled into four columns each, with a double line at the top for the date and the heading. Bentham used these sheets to jot down ideas, general principles, potential subjects for consideration, sketch out the contents of a work or to make a plan of it. These sheets are very rarely published in the new edition, but are extremely useful in indicating the genesis of a particular work, the sources which Bentham used, and the themes which he intended to address. Moreover, Bentham would often jot down a series of plans for a work, which show how the structure of the work was conceived at various points in its drafting, and provide an invaluable clue as to how to reconstruct the work.

(e) *Collectanea.* When Bentham saw items in books or newspapers or other printed or manuscript sources which interested him, he would instruct an amanuensis to copy the passage(s) in question. Bentham called this material his *collectanea*, and would often refer to it when composing a related work.

(f) *Spencers.* Many of the manuscripts are found in paper wrappers, which Bentham termed 'spencers', on which he inscribed a descriptive heading. The headings are sometimes detailed and specific, where the number of manuscripts is small and they comprise one continuous sequence, and at other times more general, where the number of manuscripts is larger and the content more wide ranging. These wrappers seem to have been used by Bentham as a rough contents index, allowing him to find and organize his material more easily. However, some of the wrappers have been misplaced, and are not always a reliable guide to the content of the material they enfold.

(g) *Correspondence.* The Bentham Papers contain a significant collection of Bentham's correspondence, both original letters which Bentham received, and drafts and copies of letters which he sent (often the only record of the letter in question).

As he composed a text, Bentham would write several drafts of the same section or chapter, write new sections, split old sections into parts and discard other sections. Each sequence of manuscript has to be located in its proper place in terms of the order in which the text was written: in other words, we need to understand the way in which Bentham, at any given time, envisaged that the text might appear. This is perhaps the most difficult, and most important, stage in the editorial process. In order to reconstruct Bentham's text, various categories of manuscripts need to be related to each other. These might include text sheets, copies of text sheets, marginal summary sheets and plans. The editor needs to know which sheets were written at a particular time, or carry the same heading, or carry a particular sequence of marginal summary paragraphs or page numbers, in order to locate them within the process of drafting.

We endeavour to publish the most mature version of the text as Bentham intended it. Earlier drafts of particular sections, for instance, will be excluded in favour of the latest draft. Given that we do not publish any sheets other than text sheets, unless there is a special reason to do so (a piece of text, for instance, which exists only in the hand of a copyist), and that a significant proportion of text sheets are often superseded by later drafts, we will typically use less than half the manuscripts related to a particular work. While the scope of the edition is comprehensive in the sense that we aim to publish every coherent work which Bentham composed, with the exception of the correspondence as noted above, it is not intended to be complete in the sense of reproducing every manuscript which he wrote.

I will illustrate the process of constructing the text by reference to the volume titled *Colonies, Commerce, and Constitutional Law: Rid Yourselves of Ultramaria and Other Writings on Spain and Spanish America*, in which Bentham, writing in 1820–2, exhorted the Spanish to grant independence to their colonies. The relevant material consisted of around 1,200 folios which were headed 'Emancipation Spanish' and 'Rid Yourselves of Ultramaria'. When I began detailed editorial work I discovered that, despite the different titles, all the material belonged to the same work, but that Bentham decided to change the title from the former to the latter in October 1820. However, it became apparent that the work went through three main stages in the course of its composition, each with discrete bodies of manuscript. In the spring and early summer of 1820 Bentham wrote the essay 'Emancipation Spanish'. He then wrote an abridgement of this work, 'Summary of Emancipate Your Colonies', which grew to be almost as long as the original work. He then began the process of redrafting which produced the final version of the work, 'Rid Yourselves of Ultramaria'. As each of these stages yielded a coherent and independent text, I decided to publish all three essays. Even so, around only 40 per cent of the total manuscripts were published in the new volume.

I hope that this gives some indication as to the way in which we go about establishing a text which is based on manuscript. Other texts, of course, are based on a printed source. Where Bentham himself saw a text through the press, we take that version to be authoritative. The editorial task might be rendered more problematic, or at least more complex, if a manuscript version of the text also survived. However, as I have already mentioned, it was Bentham's practice to destroy the manuscripts for a work which he himself had printed. So, for instance, we have virtually no surviving manuscript for *An Introduction to the Principles of Morals of Legislation.* Had such manuscript survived, there would have been a case for producing some sort of parallel edition, as the editors of the *Collected Works of John Stuart Mill* produced for Mill's *Autobiography.*[14]

We take a different approach where the printed text was seen through the press, not by Bentham himself, but by an editor, usually one of his 'disciples'. It should be noted that, with the exception up to a point of Dumont, Bentham had little active involvement in the production of such edited versions of his works. Bentham would hand over his manuscripts to the editor, and once the editorial work had been completed, he would usually ensure that the manuscripts were returned to him. In this case, he would not destroy the manuscripts. Where the text has been edited by one of Bentham's contemporaries, we do not treat the printed text as authoritative, but rather the manuscript, and hence the work in question will be based on a manuscript source, and will be edited as such.

There is, therefore, a hierarchy of sources for Bentham texts: (1) editions printed and published by Bentham himself; (2) works based on original manuscripts (preferring later drafts over earlier and originals over copies); (3) works edited during Bentham's lifetime by 'disciples'; and (4) other sources (for instance, works edited for the Bowring edition). The problem is that scholars of Bentham have not been sufficiently aware of the different status which should be accorded to the various texts, in terms of what might and might not be 'authentic' Bentham. In this context it is worth remarking that Isaiah Berlin, one of the most influential historians of philosophy in the latter half of the twentieth century, seems to have based his knowledge of Bentham on C. K. Ogden's edition of *The Theory of Legislation*, published in 1931.[15] This work was a reprint of Richard Hildreth's translation into English of Dumont's *Traités de législation civile et pénale* – a translation which had first appeared in 1864. Ogden's justification for using Hildreth's translation was that it 'has so long been a classic that it has become almost an integral part of the Bentham canon'.[16] For Berlin, it *was* the Bentham canon. Yet Dumont's work was itself, to say the least, a very liberal translation of manuscripts which Bentham had written in the 1770s and 1780s. At such a remove from the author, it seems difficult to justify its claim to be 'an integral part of the Bentham canon'.

ÉTIENNE DUMONT – EDITOR AND INTERPRETER

It is worth saying a little more about Dumont, who is the best known and most important editor of Bentham. As we have seen, Dumont produced five major French recensions of Bentham's work between 1802 and 1828. Despite the historical importance of these texts in making known Bentham's ideas, they are not being included in the new edition (an exception has been *Political Tactics*, where the only surviving version of much of the text is that of Dumont). Rather, we are returning to the original manuscripts to produce the texts as Bentham himself intended them to appear. A good example in this respect is the so-called 'Book of Fallacies', the content of which will be discussed in more detail in Chapter Five.[17] This work presents an important and highly original analysis of fallacious political arguments, the motives which give rise to their employment, and the measures which can be taken to counteract them. It is a study of the relationship between political rhetoric and political reality, and the way in which a perverse use of the former obscures the latter, and thus serves corrupt ends and sinister interests. Bentham defined a fallacy as 'a discourse designed to produce false beliefs'. Rather than being merely concerned with logical errors, he was interested in the broader question of the social and political impact of various categories of rhetorical argument. Bentham's underlying purpose in *Political Fallacies* was to expose the use of fallacious argument in defending and promoting policies and legislation, and other political acts, which were detrimental to the general welfare, and in preventing the implementation of those which would benefit it. Beyond this, he aimed to lay bare the sinister interests of those who employed such arguments.

Some of Bentham's manuscripts on this topic first appeared in French translation as 'Traité des sophismes politiques' in *Tactiques des assemblées législatives*, a two-volume recension of Bentham's writings published in 1816 by Dumont. A more substantial English version, under the title *The Book of Fallacies*, likewise based on Bentham's original manuscripts, was edited and published in 1824 by Peregrine Bingham, the barrister and legal writer. This version was reproduced in the Bowring edition.[18] A version which follows Bingham's edition but modernizes Bentham's prose, edited by Harrold A. Larrabee, appeared as *Bentham's Handbook of Political Fallacies*, in 1952 (republished 1962). A new French translation of the Larrabee edition, edited by Jean-Pierre Cléro, titled 'Manuel de sophismes politiques', appeared in 1996. All these editions are defective in that they ignore Bentham's own organization of the text. The work grew out of Bentham's interest in parliamentary reform: he assigned the fallacies which he identified to the parliamentary groups by which they were typically used, and organized the work accordingly. There were, therefore, fallacies used by government or the 'ins', those used by the opposition or the 'outs', and those used by both government and opposition, which Bentham termed fallacies of the 'eithersides'. Both Dumont and Bingham attempted to impose what they considered to be a more abstract framework on the text, and thereby give it a wider appeal, but only succeeded in obscuring Bentham's purpose. In the new edition Bentham will be allowed to speak for himself. A faithful reconstruction of the text as he intended it will not only present his ideas in their most coherent form, but will provide the most appropriate foundation for contemporary reflection upon it. In short, an authoritative edition, faithful to Bentham's own intentions, is vital for proper appreciation of the work.

CONSTRUCTING THE CANON

The new edition of *Political Fallacies* will not only be authoritative, in the sense that it will reflect Bentham's own intentions
for the work, but will produce a new text which, in one sense or
another, will become part of the canon. Another example of the
way in which the Bentham Project is constructing the canon, or
rather reconstituting the canon, through its editing of texts, is the
essay 'Nonsense upon Stilts', which I have mentioned several times
above, and has hitherto been known as 'Anarchical Fallacies'. This
essay contains the famous statement that 'Natural rights is simple
nonsense: natural and imprescriptible rights, rhetorical nonsense,
nonsense upon stilts.'[19] It is a vigorous and sustained attack on the
French Declaration of the Rights of Man originally issued in 1789,
on parts of the Declaration of the Rights and Duties of Man issued
in 1795, and on parts of a draft Declaration of Rights written by
Emmanuel Sieyès in the summer of 1789.

Bentham appears to have made no attempt to print, publish
or otherwise circulate this work at the time of its composition in
1795. In late 1797 or early 1798 he did offer the essay to Dumont for
inclusion in the work which in 1802 would be published as *Traités
de législation civile et pénale*. Dumont, however, refused to use it,
according to Bentham's later recollection, 'for fear of giving offence
to *Sieyes* etc.' In 1801 Bentham may have offered it to Cobbett for his
anti-Gallican newspaper *The Porcupine*, or failing that to the *Anti-
Jacobin Review*, but it appeared in neither. In the end it was Dumont
who, despite his earlier refusal, produced the first published version
of the essay as part of *Tactique des assemblées législatives* which
appeared in 1816. Dumont translated the essay into French, and gave
it the title 'Sophismes anarchiques'. This title was not Bentham's
own title, but it was one which it suited Dumont's purpose to adopt.
The first volume of *Tactique* contained 'Tactique des assemblées
délibérantes', Dumont's translation of 'Essays on Political Tactics',
while the second was devoted to 'sophismes'. Dumont explained that
he had included the 'sophismes' or fallacies with the 'tactique' on the
grounds that the latter influenced the form of the debates in a representative assembly, while the former influenced their substance.[20]
He had then divided the 'sophismes' into 'sophismes politiques'
and 'sophismes anarchiques'. The material for the latter was, of
course, taken from 'Nonsense upon Stilts'. Hence Dumont was able

to present his recension as a coherent and connected whole, even though it contained three different works. However, the story turns out to be more complex. While the title 'sophismes anarchiques' was not Bentham's, the phrase 'anarchical fallacies' was his. It occurs in a passage intended for *Political Fallacies*:

> Of the term *Anarchical Fallacies* the import will present itself to view as not standing too much in need of explanation.
>
> To this common head may be referred divers ways, if not of arguing, of speaking, the truth and propriety of which being admitted, it would follow that government is a bad institution, and one that, if at all, ought not for any length of time to be submitted to and endured.

When editing this material for 'Sophismes politiques', Dumont may well have seen the phrase 'anarchical fallacies', and adopted it accordingly for the critique of the French Declaration of Rights.

An English version of the work, edited by Richard Smith (about whom we know nothing, except that he was one of Bentham's most prolific editors), had to await the publication of the Bowring edition. Smith used the title 'Anarchical Fallacies', presumably translating Dumont's title, though the text of the essay was based on the original manuscripts, rather than on a retranslation of Dumont's text into English. Bowring commented that Dumont 'had considerably modified' Bentham's original text, and had 'moulded it to the state of continental society', whereas Smith's version 'may justly be said to vindicate the reputation of [Bentham's] logical powers from the aspect they assume in the feeble version of Dumont'.[21] Despite Bowring's endorsement, Smith's version is itself defective in a number of ways, which there is no need to detail here. The point is that the work has entered the canon under the title of 'Anarchical Fallacies', yet this was not Bentham's title. Indeed, by Bentham's own definition of a fallacy, the Declaration of Rights does not seem to have constituted a fallacy – a fallacy was a delusive argument, whereas a Declaration of Rights as such did not, and was not intended to, present an argument. The full title of the essay as published in the new edition is

> Nonsense upon Stilts, or Pandora's Box Opened, or the French Declaration of Rights prefixed to the Constitution of 1791 laid

open and exposed – with a comparative sketch of what has been done on the same subject in the Constitution of 1795, and a sample of Citizen Sieyès.

Bentham put forward a number of alternative titles at the time of the composition of the work, but this was chosen as it represented most accurately the scope of the essay and the way in which Bentham intended it to be organized. Having said that, I was tempted by the following alternative: 'No French Nonsense: or, A Cross-Buttock for the first Declaration of Rights: together with a Kick of the A – for the second: by a practitioner of the Old English Art of self-Defence.'

RE-EDITING *OF LAWS IN GENERAL*

Finally, I will illustrate the value of adopting a historical approach, and more particularly an approach which gives priority to authorial intention, in constructing the text. It is important not to conflate texts written at different times, and possibly for different purposes, even though they deal with the same subject-matter, and might even carry the same heading. The strategy of the editors of the Bowring edition was to take what they conceived to be writings related to the same subject, and to combine them into one work, without paying much regard to the period at which, or the purpose for which, the manuscripts had been written. The results have been, in many cases, to make Bentham appear a far less coherent thinker than he actually was: paradoxically, the attempt to impose coherence tends to result in incoherence. But instead of taking the Bowring edition for my target, which is not easy to miss, let me take H. L. A. Hart's edition of *Of Laws in General*, one of the early volumes in the new *Collected Works*. Incidentally, this work itself only became known after its 'discovery' and first publication by C. W. Everett in 1945.[22] Hart has expressed the view that, had it been known in the nineteenth century, the course of English jurisprudence would have been significantly altered for the better.[23]

It is no secret that Hart's edition of *Of Laws in General* contains over 1,000 errors of transcription, and that a Corrigenda had to be issued. The claim is made in the Corrigenda that the corrections are all of a minor nature. I was asked to help prepare a second edition of *Of Laws in General* for publication in paperback. Just in case any problems remained, I decided to check a portion of the text against the original manuscript. One thing led to another, and instead of a second edition incorporating the corrections identified in the Corrigenda, I have in effect re-edited the text, making major revisions and restoring Bentham's original title, namely *Of the Limits of the Penal Branch of Jurisprudence*. There are a significant number of transcription errors which have not been corrected in the Corrigenda, and serious problems with the internal ordering of many of the chapters. But I will concentrate here on one substantive point which has emerged from this editorial work and which concerns Bentham's conception of constitutional law. Scholars have disagreed over the nature of Bentham's understanding of constitutional law, with two crucial passages which appear in *Of Laws in General* at the centre of the controversy. In one passage Bentham seems to agree with the view he had earlier put forward in *A Fragment on Government* (and later made famous by John Austin) that constitutional law was not properly law, but rather a form of positive morality. In a second passage he seems to say that constitutional law is properly understood as law since it emanates from the sovereign like all other law, distinguishing between law *in principem*, that is, law addressed to the sovereign, and law *in populum*, that is, law addressed to the people. Law *in principem* is enforced by the moral or religious sanction, rather than by the political sanction.[24] As the text appears in *Of Laws in General*, both passages have equal status – both appear to represent Bentham's thinking at one particular point of time, and the inclination is to try to find a way of reconciling them. What the editor of *Of Laws in General* has failed to tell the reader is that one passage was written at a slightly later date, and represents, in Bentham's own mind, a new departure in his thought. This is shown by the fact that Bentham has added two marginal comments to the manuscript containing the passage written at the earlier date. The first comment appertains to the following portion of this earlier passage:

> In the definition that hath just been given of a legal mandate it follows that the mandate of the sovereign be it what it will, cannot be illegal: it may be cruel; it may be impolitic; it may even be unconstitutional: but it cannot be illegal. It may be unconstitutional, for instance by being repugnant to any privileges that may have been conceded to the people whom it affects: but it

would be perverting language and confounding ideas to call it *illegal*: for concessions of privileges are not mandates: they are neither commands nor countermands: in short they are not *laws*. They are only promises from the sovereign to the people that he will not issue any law, any mandate, any command or countermand but to such or such an effect, or perhaps with the concurrence of such or such persons.[25]

In the margin, Bentham has commented: 'Alter. These are laws not *in populum* indeed, but *in principem*.'[26] The second comment appertains to the following portion of this same passage:

The principal contents of the Imperial capitulations are either concessions of privileges or treaties according to the relation which the Emperor is considered as bearing at the several periods to the other states. I would not, without examining them in this particular view, be sure of their containing any matter of the mandative kind.[27]

In the margin here, Bentham has commented: 'They are *leges in principem* in which the party favoured is either a subject or co-imperant or an independent prince.'[28] As Bentham was working on this text, he discovered or invented the distinction between law *in populum* and law *in principem*, and thereby superseded his earlier analysis of the nature of constitutional law.

This example shows precisely why the Bentham edition needs to be based on a minutely detailed historical study of Bentham's manuscripts. The method I have adopted when editing texts is to reconstruct them as closely as possible to Bentham's intentions at the time of writing, but to recognize that Bentham's intentions might well change during the course of drafting a particular work. The work whose short working title was successively 'Emancipation Spanish' and 'Rid Yourselves of Ultramaria', which I have discussed above, is an especially pertinent example of the benefits of adopting such an approach. A different approach (the approach which the editors of the Bowring edition would have adopted had they bothered to edit this material) would have been to take the whole body of manuscripts, extract what the editor considered to be the most interesting or coherent parts, and produce one work under one title or the other. My study of the manuscripts revealed that there were actually three virtually distinct works, admittedly somewhat repetitive in their content, but with almost totally distinct bodies of manuscript. By reconstructing Bentham's conception of the work at each successive point in time, it proved possible to create three coherent texts, and show the way in which Bentham's thinking had evolved.

Another result of this historical approach is to reveal connections between works which may not have previously been appreciated. Take, for example, the proposed contents of the new *Collected Works* edition of Bentham's economic writings. Under the original plan drawn up at the outset of the edition,[29] it was decided that one of the volumes of economic writings would contain the pamphlet published in 1821 as *Observations on the Restrictive and Prohibitory Commercial System*. In the course of editing the volume on Spain and Spanish America, it became clear to me that this work was originally intended as an appendix to one of the sections in 'Rid Yourselves of Ultramaria'. Its link in terms of provenance, chronology and theme to 'Rid Yourselves of Ultramaria' meant that the proper place for it was in *Colonies, Commerce, and Constitutional Law*. For similar reasons *Emancipate Your Colonies!*, printed early in 1793 but not published until 1830, has been included in the volume of writings on the French Revolution, rather than in one of the volumes of economic writings.[30] Of course, a projected volume on colonies, which would have included all these essays, together with some other material, has disappeared. The scholar who would, for the sake of convenience, like to have all of Bentham's writings on colonies collected into one volume will find compensation in the greater potential for understanding the historical context of each work and the historical development of Bentham's thought more generally.

BENEFITS OF THE NEW EDITION

I will emphasize several points in conclusion. First, the new Bentham edition is far superior to previous editions, judged by the standard of reconstructing the texts according to Bentham's intentions. Second, better texts (and I refer here both to the text itself and to the accompanying annotation) give rise to better scholarship, as evidenced by the excellence of much of the recent literature which draws on the *Collected Works* volumes. Third, the indexes which accompany the new texts allow particular topics to be studied more comprehensively (note here, for instance, the stimulus given to students of John Stuart Mill by the cumulative index produced for the new Toronto edition of Mill's *Collected Works*).[31] Fourth, editors should, in their editorial introductions, state openly and comprehensively how they have gone about their task, and scholars should be prepared to read such introductions in order to gain a proper appreciation of the status of the text which they are reading. And fifth, in answer to the question 'Which Bentham?', in what follows I have relied where possible first, on works published in the new authoritative edition; second, on works published by Bentham himself (although, for ease of reference, I have used the versions reprinted in the Bowring edition); and third, on transcriptions of the original manuscripts. The Bentham I aim to present is the 'authenticity' Bentham. While I have been prescriptive about how one should edit Bentham's texts, I am entirely permissive about the sort of approach the scholar or commentator might adopt. That will depend upon the discipline and the purpose. I have drawn attention to three prominent approaches to the study of texts – in brief those which concentrate on philosophical insight, on author's meaning and on historical context. In what follows I adopt each approach at various points, though in Chapters Three and Seven the first approach is predominant, and in Chapters Four, Five and Six the second. Each chapter will deal with some important and perplexing aspect of Bentham's thought, and together will maintain, at least until Chapter Seven, some sense of chronology.

CHAPTER THREE

THE PRINCIPLE OF UTILITY

UTILITY

Bentham's best-known work is *An Introduction to the Principles of Morals and Legislation*, which, like many of his texts, has a complicated history. As we have already noted, it was first printed in 1780, but not published until 1789. A second edition, with some additional material, appeared in 1823. It constitutes the first part (not the whole) of an introduction to a much larger project – a complete penal code. Bentham had originally intended to include several further chapters, including one on the limits between law and morals and one on indirect legislation (whereas direct legislation commanded or prohibited certain actions, indirect legislation established the conditions in which particular actions were either encouraged or discouraged), but these chapters themselves grew into book-length studies.[1] The work begins with the most frequently quoted paragraph in all of Bentham's corpus, in which he explains, in language which he himself dismisses as 'metaphor and declamation', that the foundational principles both of psychology and of ethics are derived from the sensations of pleasure and pain:

> Nature has placed mankind under the governance of two sovereign masters, *pain* and *pleasure*. It is for them alone to point out what we ought to do, as well as to determine what we shall do. On the one hand the standard of right and wrong, on the other the chain of causes and effects, are fastened to their throne. They govern us in all we do, in all we say, in all we think: every effort we can make to throw off our subjection, will serve but to demonstrate and confirm it. In words a man may pretend to

abjure their empire: but in reality he will remain subject to it all the while. The *principle of utility* recognises this subjection, and assumes it for the foundation of that system, the object of which is to rear the fabric of felicity by the hands of reason and of law. Systems which attempt to question it, deal in sounds instead of sense, in caprice instead of reason, in darkness instead of light.[2]

The 'sovereign masters' of pain and pleasure not only directed human action – 'govern[ing] us in all we do, in all we say, in all we think' – but also indicated 'the standard of right and wrong'. They constituted not only the foundation of human psychology, determining what individuals actually did, but also the foundation of ethics, pointing out what they ought to do. Hence, psychology and ethics were linked by their relation to pleasure and pain. The key to understanding Bentham's principle of utility is to understand the way in which both what is done and what it is morally right to do are dependent upon the sensations of pleasure and pain.

In Bentham's view, the desire for pleasure and the aversion to pain lie at the root of all human action – indeed they lie at the root of the action of all sentient creatures. What matter, in the sense of what are important, are the sensations of pain and pleasure, and not, for instance, whether one possesses a rational faculty or some supernatural entity such as a soul. From this perspective, the welfare of animals is no less important than that of human beings, and must be taken into account: 'the question is not, Can they *reason*? nor, Can they *talk*? but, Can they *suffer*?'[3] Now, to suffer is to experience pain, just as to enjoy or to be happy is to experience pleasure. Words such as suffering and happiness do not make any sense unless they are explained by their relationship to the sensations of pain and pleasure. In the same way, in the field of ethics, the terms good and evil make no sense unless they are explained in terms of pleasure and pain respectively: '*Good* is pleasure or exemption from pain . . . *Evil* is pain or loss of pleasure.'[4] To say that pleasure and pain lie at the root of the actions of sentient creatures is to say that such creatures are motivated by a desire for pleasure and an aversion to pain. And to say this is to say that motives consist in a desire for pleasure and an aversion to pain – in other words, actions are motivated by the prospect of obtaining some pleasure or of averting some pain. If an individual will gain pleasure from performing some action or seeing some state of affairs brought into existence,

he is said to have an interest in performing that action or in bring-
ing about that state of affairs. In order for an action to take place,
the agent must have the relevant desire (and, once again, the notion
of desire makes no sense without reference to pleasure) coupled
with the relevant power – or conceive himself to have the power –
to achieve his objective. To put this another way, for an action to
take place, the desire or will has to be combined with the power.
The will, as a faculty of the human mind, is directed, at least where
no coercion is involved, by the understanding, which itself consists
in knowledge and judgement. But even though, when we act, it is
our intention to increase our pleasure and to reduce or eliminate
our pain, Bentham recognizes that we will not always be successful,
because we may act on inadequate or incorrect information, or may
simply make a poor choice because of a defect in our judgement. An
inquisitive young child, for instance, may be attracted by the flick-
ering flame of a candle, and put out his finger to touch it, expecting
to gain pleasure from the experience. Unfortunately, he has made
a mistake, and howls with pain when he burns himself. In order for
the action to be successful in the sense of achieving a desired out-
come, the agent must have the relevant and necessary knowledge
and judgement. In our example, the child lacks the knowledge he
needs about the relationship between flame, heat and flesh to prevent him from burning his finger.

The pursuit of our own happiness is not, however, the right and
proper course of action. A right and proper action is one that promotes 'the greatest happiness of the greatest number'.[5] But how is
it psychologically possible for an individual to pursue the greatest
happiness of the greatest number, given that he is motivated by a
desire to increase his own happiness? Before considering this question, I will deal with the criticism that Bentham advocates an egotistical or self-centred theory of ethics – in other words, he claims, say
the critics, that an individual acts in the right way when he attempts
to maximize his own happiness without regard to the happiness of
others. On this view, Bentham, it is assumed, accepts that if each
individual acts in this way, it will turn out for the best overall. To
brand an ethical theory egotistical or selfish seems, in the eyes of
these critics, to be enough to condemn it, but this merely begs the
question. It is necessary to show what is wrong with an egotistical
theory. Having said that, the short answer to these critics is that
Bentham's theory, as we shall see, is not egotistical, and, moreover,

Bentham does in fact attempt to show what is wrong with egotism. He performs this latter task through his 'axioms of mental pathology'. It should be noted that by 'pathology' Bentham does not mean the study of disease, but rather adopts a less common meaning of the term whereby it refers to the study of the emotions, passions or feelings. By axiom, he means propositions which cannot be 'proved' by reference to more general propositions, but which we will accept as true when we reflect upon our own experience. One such axiom of mental pathology is that the suffering produced by loss is greater than the happiness produced by gain.[6] Your pocket has been picked, and you lose £20. On the other hand, the pickpocket has gained £20. The money will buy the same quantity of goods for the pickpocket as it would have bought for you. It seems that there is no change overall, in that the pain you feel at the loss is evened out by the pleasure the pickpocket feels at the gain. Bentham, however, claims that the pain felt at the loss outweighs the pleasure felt by the gain. This example illustrates two important points. The first is that where there is a clash between the interests of one individual and those of another, the increase of the happiness of the one will be at the expense of the happiness of the other. The second is that the presumption must be that the loss of happiness, or the active suffering produced, on the part of the disadvantaged individual will outweigh the gain on the part of the advantaged individual. Bentham has shown why the pursuit by each of his own happiness – in other words egotism – is wrong, insofar as there exists a clash of interests, in that it will result in an overall balance on the side of misery and suffering.

To return to the question: how is it psychologically possible for an individual to pursue the greatest happiness? This is where the legislator steps in. Indeed, it is Bentham's purpose in *An Introduction to the Principles of Morals and Legislation* to show the legislator how to accomplish his objective – or rather what Bentham assumes no legislator can deny is his proper objective – the promotion of the happiness of the members of the community subject to him.[7] In order to ensure that individuals act in such a way as to promote the greatest happiness, that is, produce the maximum of pleasure and the minimum of pain within the community as a whole, they have to be provided with appropriate motives, themselves composed of pain and pleasure. Whatever it is that is to be done, states Bentham, 'there is nothing by which a man can ultimately be *made* to do it, but either pain or pleasure'. Once the 'subjection' of human beings to the 'two sovereign masters' has been recognized, a key is provided not only to the production of action, but also to the production of action of the right kind. The legislator, therefore, uses rewards and punishments in order to encourage and to discourage particular actions.

In distributing reward and punishment – in other words, pleasure and pain – the legislator imposes a sanction. As well as referring to the reward and punishment so imposed, Bentham uses the term sanction to refer to a 'source' of pleasure and pain. In *An Introduction to the Principles of Morals and Legislation* he identifies three such sources corresponding to the person or persons who are supposed to impose the pleasure and pain in question. The political, including the legal, sanction is imposed by the judge, acting in accordance with the declared will of the sovereign in the state. The moral or popular sanction is imposed by members of the public, acting in an informal capacity. In his mature constitutional theory, Bentham places great reliance on the moral or popular sanction, operating through the 'Public Opinion Tribunal', as a counterforce to the sinister interest of rulers. Finally, the religious sanction is imposed, either in the present or a future life, by a supernatural being.[8] If you drive your car dangerously, and are prosecuted, the fine you receive from the judge will constitute the political, including the legal, sanction; the condemnation you receive from the editor of the local newspaper which reports the incident, and from your family and friends, will constitute the moral or popular sanction; and the punishment you receive from God on account of your sin will represent the religious sanction.

Returning to the example of the pickpocket, we saw how, all other things being equal, the pickpocket's gain is outweighed by your loss. But let us look at the situation from the perspective of the pickpocket. He steals your money because he has calculated that, as far as he is concerned, it is beneficial for him to do so. Yet, overall, the theft produces more pain than pleasure, and is, therefore, wrong. The legislator, committed to the promotion of the greatest happiness of the community, sees that it is better for individuals not to have their pockets picked. He introduces a law which states that pickpocketing is an offence, and any person committing it will suffer a punishment. He also introduces a police force for the detection and arrest of offenders. Looking at the situation again from the perspective of the pickpocket, he now calculates that if he picks your pocket, the likelihood is that he will be detected, and then subjected to punishment. He decides that the potential gain is not worth the risk. The legislator has altered the behaviour of the pickpocket by applying a sanction to the action which, were it not for the sanction and the chance of detection, he would have undertaken. Place the whole field of legislation on a utilitarian basis, and the individual no longer has any incentive to perform actions which are detrimental to the community as a whole. He is left free to pursue his own interest insofar as it causes no detriment to others, and insofar as it proves beneficial to others.

In order to achieve his objective, the legislator, says Bentham, not only has to understand that he must operate through pain and pleasure – in the form of punishment and reward – he has also to understand the 'force' or 'value' of different pains and pleasures.[9] In short, a more valuable pleasure is a pleasure of greater quantity. The value of a pleasure or pain, as far as a single individual is concerned, is estimated by reference to six 'elements' or 'dimensions', namely its intensity, duration, certainty or uncertainty, propinquity or remoteness, fecundity, and purity. Laying pain to one side for the moment, the intensity of a pleasure refers to its subjective strength; duration refers to the length of time for which the pleasure is experienced; certainty refers to the likelihood of the pleasure being experienced; propinquity refers to the point in time at which the pleasure will begin to be experienced; fecundity refers to the likelihood of the pleasure leading to further sensations of pleasure; and purity to the likelihood of the pleasure not leading to sensations of pain – for instance, the pleasure of inebriation is impure in that it will be followed by the painful sensation known as a 'hangover'. Where the value of a pleasure or pain is considered in relation to more than one person, then in addition to these six elements, the element of extent, that is the number of persons affected by it, has also to be taken into account. Bentham explains the method for coming to 'an exact account . . . of the general tendency of any act, by which the interests of a community are affected'. Calculate the good or evil tendency of an act by means of balancing the value of the pleasures and pains produced in the instance of a single individual; repeat the process for each individual affected; and, finally, aggregate the results.

Take the *balance*; which, if on the side of *pleasure*, will give the general *good tendency* of the act, with respect to the total number of community of individuals concerned; if on the side of pain, the general *evil tendency*, with respect to the same community.[10]

To return to our example of the pickpocket, the legislator, estimating the value of the pleasures and pains produced by the action of the pickpocket, recognizes that the action is detrimental to the greatest happiness, and therefore attaches not merely a random punishment or sanction to it, but one which will be nicely calculated to alter the motives of the potential pickpocket at the least possible expense in terms of punishment – too little punishment will be ineffective, while too much will be unnecessary and self-defeating from a utilitarian point of view. This method forms the basis for a rational penal code. Actions which are detrimental to happiness should be constituted into offences, while those which harm no one should be left alone – a principle which would, for instance, have led in Bentham's time to the decriminalizing of a whole series of religious and sexual offences.

It is worth noting that by the appearance of the second edition of *An Introduction to the Principles of Morals and Legislation* in 1823, Bentham had come to prefer the phrase 'the greatest happiness principle' or 'the greatest felicity principle' instead of 'the principle of utility'. The term 'utility' did not sufficiently convey the idea of happiness. Moreover, the new formulation, unlike the original one, gave an indication of the number of the interests involved, for it was the number which was 'the circumstance, which contributes, in the largest proportion, to the formation of the standard here in question; the *standard of right and wrong* by which alone the propriety of human conduct, in every situation, can with propriety be tried'.[11] Bentham's preference for the new formulation may not be unrelated to his conversion to political radicalism.

LOGIC AND LANGUAGE

It is often assumed that the starting-point for Bentham's thought is the principle of utility. There is, however, a deeper aspect to his thought, on which the principle of utility itself is founded. This is his ontology, and the theory of logic and language which is linked to it. Bentham did not himself publish a major work on this subject – although poorly edited texts did appear in the Bowring edition – but there is no doubt that his views were formed extremely early in life, probably during his teenage years, and before he invented his version of the principle of utility in 1769. The radical ontological question is – what exists?[12] Bentham's answer is – substance. Or to put the question more subtly, given that we, as human beings, are limited to our five senses, what do we perceive to exist? The answer – the physical world. If anything which is not substance – which is not part of the physical world – has existence, then it cannot be known to human beings. The supernatural (or what, for Bentham, amounts to the same thing, the metaphysical) is unknowable; and any proposition concerning it is subject neither to verification nor to falsification – it is nonsense. Even knowledge of the physical world is problematic to the extent that the human mind does not perceive that world directly, but rather its perceptions of that world. It is conceivable that our physiology systematically distorts the physical world. This is not the equivalent of a mere mistake: for instance, I hear a noise outside my window and think that it is raining, but when I look out, I see that the wind is rustling the leaves in a nearby tree. In this case, the mistaken interpretation of my perception (my mistaken judgement) is rectified by further observation. In the case of our perceptions of the physical world in general, there is no means of ascertaining whether a systematic distortion is taking place. But if so, notes Bentham, it is of no practical concern whatsoever, so we may as well just assume that what we perceive *is* the physical world.

Our perceptions of the physical world lodge themselves in our minds, where they are processed. In other words, we think – but thinking, and communication of thought, is done by and through language. So there is no matter of greater importance (in other words no matter which more influences our well-being or happiness) than the way in which language is used to describe the physical world. For Bentham, the fundamental distinction in language, as we have seen in Chapter One,[13] is between the names of real entities – which represent objects existing in the physical world (for instance, an apple or a table) – and the names of fictitious entities – objects which are spoken about as if they do exist, and about which it makes sense to talk as though they exist, but to which we do not intend to ascribe physical existence (for instance, some property of a physical object, such as the sweetness of an apple, or an abstraction, such as a law or an obligation). There are other types of 'entity' in Bentham's scheme, but these are ultimately explicable in no other way than by relation to real and fictitious entities – for instance, a fabulous entity, such as a unicorn, consists in a combination of real entities which has never been perceived in the physical world, but exists in imagination, while a nonentity consists in an absence of substance, or, put another way, in an absence of any real entity.

In order to make sense, language has to refer, either directly or indirectly, to physical objects. A major advance which Bentham believed he had made was in the discovery of a method by which the names of fictitious entities can be related to their 'real source' in the physical world. The names of fictitious entities are not capable of exposition by means of representation, where a specific object is produced and its assigned name pronounced, for there is no such object to produce. You can produce an apple (a real entity), and explain to a person that the object is called an apple. But you cannot produce a physical object and explain to a person that the object is called an obligation, or a right, or a power – or at least do so and be considered to be talking sense. Nor is it possible to define a fictitious entity by means of the Aristotelian method of definition *per genus et differentiam*. Definition by this means is possible where the object belongs to a nest of aggregates, but is not possible where the word has no superior genus. An apple, it might be explained, is a fruit with certain distinguishing characteristics, but an obligation is not a sort of anything.

Bentham's discovery consists in the complementary techniques of paraphrasis and phraseoplerosis. The first operation to be performed is phraseoplerosis, whereby the phrase which includes the noun requiring exposition is 'filled up'. Discourse often contains ellipses, which need to be expanded in order fully to capture the sense of the proposition in question. For instance, if I shout 'Dog!', I may mean 'There is a dog over there', or I may mean 'Beware of the dog which is about to attack you', or I may simply be insulting you. Once the relevant words have been supplied (and this might require a whole series of operations in terms of, for instance, understanding the context of the utterance and the motives of the speaker), the operation of paraphrasis can be undertaken. Paraphrasis consists in the translation of one phrase or sentence into another phrase or sentence. This is not merely to change one word for a synonym – that gets you nowhere. Nor is it merely to put the same sentence into different words. Rather, paraphrasis occurs when a sentence in which the name of the fictitious entity appears is translated into another sentence in which the words are either real entities, or are more nearly related to real entities. There is both a translation of the sentence, and a movement towards the physical. Bentham takes the notion of a person having a legal duty as an illustration. A person (X) has a legal duty when someone else (Y) has a right to have him (X) made to perform it, in which case X has a duty towards Y, and Y a right against X. From here, we can state that what Y has a legal right to have X be made to do is that for which X is legally liable, upon a requisition made on Y's behalf, to be punished for not doing.[14] The definition or exposition has 'resolved' the notion of duty into its simple, or more simple, elements: namely, the prospect of suffering a punishment (a term which itself will require further exposition), upon the forbearance to perform some action, when required to do so by the person invested with the corresponding right.

However, if an exposition by paraphrasis proves to be impossible, then the fictitious entity in question belongs to the class of nonentities, the noun substantive by which it is represented is merely a sound, and any proposition in which it occurs is nonsensical. We shall see how this plays out when we discuss Bentham's attitude to religion and to natural rights.[15] The immediate point is that the principle of utility is a fictitious entity. There is no physical object which we can produce and say, 'this thing is the principle of utility'. But we can undertake an exposition of the term 'the principle of utility' by the technique of paraphrasis. We will then see that an adherent of 'the principle of utility' is a person who approves of that action which promotes the greatest happiness of the greatest number, and that happiness consists in a balance of pleasure over pain. If you return to the first part of this chapter, you will see that the expositions given there of terms such as good, evil, motive and interest are examples of paraphrasis, and that the real entities at the root of those expositions are pleasure and pain.

CRITICISM OF BENTHAM'S PSYCHOLOGICAL THEORY

Bentham is a psychological hedonist – in other words, he takes it to be a fact of human nature that we are motivated solely by a desire for pleasure and an aversion to pain. Many critics have argued that this is simply not a plausible explanation of human psychology. One line of criticism we have already encountered, but more needs to be said about it here. This is the view that Bentham's psychology is egotistical, and, therefore, does not account for the altruism which characterizes the conduct of some individuals – the extreme case being those persons whom we regard as 'saints', and not just in the narrow sense of those canonized by the Roman Catholic Church, but those who are distinguished by their kindness and consideration towards others. Indeed, such kindness and consideration are a feature at some point or other of many people's conduct. Bentham has a perfectly adequate response to the criticism that he cannot account for altruistic behaviour. He divides motives into three broad classes – self-regarding motives, social or sympathetic motives, and dissocial or antipathetic motives.[16] He admits that most people, most of the time, are motivated by self-regard, that is perform actions which are aimed at increasing their own happiness, but he also points out that if this were not the case, none of us would survive very long, and the species would soon be extinct.[17] A simple example will explain what he means by this. Imagine that you are sitting at a table with another person, and have a plate of food to share. If you are a purely altruistic being, you will say: 'Please, eat.' Assume that your companion is also a purely altruistic being. He will respond: 'No, after you.' To which you will reply: 'No, after you.' Eventually you will both die because neither of you will eat before the other. The reason why you do in fact eat is because you are motivated to do so by self-regard. Self-regard is, and must necessarily be, the preponderant motive or 'spring of action', taking the human species as a whole.

But human beings are also motivated by sympathetic regard, that is, they perform actions which are aimed at promoting the happiness of others. However, such actions are not 'disinterested' in the sense that the person performing them has no interest in them.[18] The sympathetic actor receives pleasure from seeing other people's pleasure increase – hence, he still promotes his own pleasure, even though his action is intended to benefit someone else. How can it be otherwise? A person cannot feel another person's pleasure – only his own. As we have seen, a motive is necessary for an action to take place (a motiveless action is a solecism), and a motive consists of some desire for pleasure or aversion to pain.

Finally, human beings may be motivated by antipathy, that is, the desire to increase the pain or suffering of some other person, because the infliction of such pain produces pleasure. When the perpetrator of a particularly horrendous crime, for instance, is brought to justice, we are likely to feel the pleasure of antipathy when he is sentenced to life imprisonment; some people would feel even more pleasure if he were sentenced to death (though not Bentham, as he strongly opposed capital punishment). To put this another way, a person will promote the pleasure of those for whom he feels sympathy, and inflict pain on those for whom he feels antipathy – he will act from motives of sympathy towards the former, and from motives of antipathy towards the latter. In short, Bentham thinks that we are predominantly motivated by self-regard or self-preference; motivated to some extent by sympathy; and motivated to the least degree by antipathy. The balance, however, will be different in different individuals – hence, there are people whom we criticize for being selfish, and others whom we praise for being benevolent. Bentham, therefore, has a perfectly adequate account of altruistic behaviour.

Another criticism of Bentham's psychology is that it is 'reductionist'. It is not clear why 'reductionism' is a bad thing, but it is what Bentham would call a 'hobgoblin' term which carries condemnation along with it. What this criticism amounts to is, once again, the view that human beings are motivated by something in addition to the desire for pleasure or the aversion to pain. No one denies that pleasure and pain are important features of human psychology, but critics argue that it is self-evidently wrong to suggest that these form the only motives. John Finnis, for instance, argues that there are seven 'basic forms of human good', which are independent ends in themselves, including the desire for knowledge, aesthetic experience, friendship and religious experience. What matters, says Finnis, is the knowledge we acquire, not the pleasure with which that acquisition might be accompanied. And so in regard to the other basic goods.[19] A similar argument is advanced by Robert Nozick with his conceit of the 'experience machine'. Nozick asks us whether we would choose to be plugged into an 'experience machine' which could be programmed to make us believe that we were undergoing certain experiences which would bring us the maximum amount of pleasure. If you want to be an astronaut and visit the Moon, the machine will be programmed to give you that experience. You will be taken out of the machine every six months, when you can choose your experiences for the next six months. Nozick argues that none of us would choose to be plugged into the machine. The machine is based on the premise that what we want is to maximize our pleasure. The fact that we would choose not to be plugged in falsifies that premise. What we do want is to be in control of our own lives – making our own choices, pursuing our own values, having our own experiences, in the real world – in other words, we want to *be*, rather than merely to *experience*.[20] The film *The Matrix* makes the same point as Nozick. The heroes want to live a 'real' life, rather than merely be programmed to have 'experiences'. There is more to life than the mere pursuit of pleasure.

In response to this criticism, let us look in a little more detail at Bentham's classification of pleasures and pains, which is in effect the same thing as his classification of motives or of desires and aversions. In *A Table of the Springs of Action* (1817), Bentham presents a list of 14 such pleasures and pains. He admits that his list is not definitive and may be subject to modification, but he believes it will be helpful to the legislator. The pleasures include those of eating and drinking, of the sexual appetite, of wealth, of the exercise of power, of curiosity, of friendship, of reputation, of religion, of sympathy, and so forth.[21] On one level, this looks very similar in conception to Finnis's list, albeit with more divisions. But for Bentham, the reason why we desire wealth or want to exercise power is simply for the pleasure which the possession of wealth or the exercise of power brings. The end is the pleasure, although different means of obtaining that pleasure will be attractive to different individuals. Hence, some individuals will prefer to acquire wealth, others will prefer to enhance their reputation, others will prefer to have sex, while others will prefer to study philosophy (not that the latter two activities are mutually exclusive, unless one adopts asceticism, but more on that in Chapter Six).[22] Bentham recognizes that different individuals will have different 'sensibilities', depending upon all sorts of physiological and sociological factors, such as the physical constitution of one's body, one's mental qualities, age, gender, the climate where one lives, the form of government under which one lives and one's religious views.[23]

Another essential feature of Bentham's psychology is the theory of the association of ideas. This was a standard feature of eighteenth-century psychology more generally, finding its classic statement in David Hartley's *Observations on Man* (1749), and later given its distinctive utilitarian statement by James Mill in *Analysis of the Phenomena of the Human Mind* (1829). The association of ideas explains, for instance, why human beings may perform actions which do not appear to maximize, or even increase, their pleasure. The key to this irrational behaviour is the influence of habit. You may, for instance, have gone to a football match at some point in the past, and genuinely enjoyed the experience, because your favourite team won the game. You go again, and your team wins again. You go time after time to the game. However, the fortunes of your team take a disastrous turn, and it loses every game. If you were to think afresh about the nature of the experience, you might realize that going to the game has become a painful, rather than a pleasurable, experience. You may then decide that you would derive more pleasure from reading a book of philosophy. You may not, however, rethink your priorities in such a way because the habit of going to the game is too strongly associated in your mind with pleasure and it is simply what you do on a particular evening. Again, you may undertake an activity, or hold a point of view, which is, in fact, detrimental to your well-being, but you accept it as necessary or inevitable. Such a state of mind may be brought about by what Bentham terms 'delusion' – a notion he developed in his later political writings to explain why an oppressed people might support an oppressing government.[24] And finally, when you make a decision as to whether to go to the football game, or whether instead to read a philosophy book, you will, if you are prudent, not take into account merely the immediate or short-term consequences of your action, but all the consequences over the longest term possible. This may lead you to sacrifice some current enjoyment for what you conceive to be a greater, but more remote, enjoyment. For instance, the immediate pleasure obtained by going out this evening with your friends to a night club and imbibing large amounts of alcohol may at first sight appear to be an appealing option, but when you reflect that tomorrow morning you will have a bad headache, which will prevent you enjoying your philosophy class, and that you can use the money you have saved to purchase a copy of Bentham's *An Introduction to the Principles of Morals and Legislation*, you will make the prudent decision – that is, the decision which will overall maximize your pleasure – and stay at home and prepare for your philosophy class.

If Bentham is correct – perhaps not about the substance of the decision you take, but about the way your mind comes to its decisions – then all the decisions you take are taken with a view to maximizing your pleasure, insofar as you are informed about the relevant consequences, and swayed to a greater or lesser extent by whatever associations of ideas have accumulated in your mind. Whether we are choosing a ham sandwich or a tuna salad sandwich for lunch, or whether we are choosing to take a course on the British utilitarians or the German idealists, or whether we are choosing a wife or husband, the only criterion which matters for us is how much pleasure we expect to receive from each available course of action. Bentham's 'reductionist' psychology turns out to have significant explanatory power. The exposition of human motivation in terms of the pursuit of pleasure and the avoidance of pain (the term 'exposition', which suggests Bentham's technique of paraphrasis, does not carry the condemnatory associations – the associations of ideas – of the term 'reduction') does not seem to be obviously wrong, even though many philosophers say that it is. But it does not matter what philosophers say. Bentham's appeal here is to our own experience. He asks us to reflect on that experience, and is confident that we will agree that, ultimately, we conceive ourselves to be motivated solely by a desire for pleasure and an aversion to pain.

The final criticism of Bentham's psychology with which I will deal here relates to the sort of calculation which, on his account, we all engage in, and which is often referred to as 'the felicific calculus', though this term does not appear in Bentham's own writing. This criticism overlaps with, and leads into, criticism of his ethical theory. The argument is that pleasures are incommensurable, and so cannot be compared in the way in which the felicific calculus demands. As far as the individual is concerned, it is impossible to make intrapersonal comparisons – in other words I cannot compare the pleasure I receive from going to the football game with the pleasure I receive from reading philosophy. As far as the community in general is concerned (and this criticism, if valid, undermines the whole of Bentham's legislative programme), it is impossible to make interpersonal comparisons – in other words the pleasure I receive from going to the football game cannot be compared with the pleasure you receive from going to the same game, and still less can the pleasure I receive from going to the game be compared with the pleasure you receive from reading philosophy. The fundamental objection here is that pleasures cannot be given any mathematical value at all. In response, it is worth noting that Bentham himself never assigned numerical values to pleasures of various kinds, but rather appealed to arguments about the benefits or costs ('burthens' in his language) which were likely to result from different courses of action. Having said that, there is no doubt that Bentham believes that numerical comparisons can be helpfully made in relation to certain of the elements of pleasure and pain. A pleasure which lasts 1 hour is half as valuable as the same pleasure which lasts 2 hours. If a pleasure is certain to follow from a particular action, then it can be given a value of 1. If it will follow in half the instances, then it can be given a value of ½. Propinquity and remoteness can be understood in terms of the interest payable on money. For instance, if I am given £100 today, and if interest rates are set at 5 per cent per annum, in one year's time the gift will be worth £105. If I am given the same £100 in one year's time, I will have lost £5. In other words, the same pleasure experienced now is worth more than the same pleasure experienced at some point in the future. Intensity is the element of pleasure to which a value cannot be ascribed, states Bentham. Intensity is idiosyncratic – since no one can experience another person's pleasure, it is impossible to know how intensely another person experiences their feelings.[25]

Does it follow from this that we can make any sense of intrapersonal comparisons of pleasure and pain? Are we able to rank different pleasures and pains in such a way that we can decide which course of action it is rational for us to pursue? An important discussion of this question has been undertaken by Tom Warke, who argues that Bentham does not claim that we put an objective value on each potential pleasure (for instance, going to the football game is worth 4.1 utils (units of utility) while reading philosophy is worth 3.7 utils), but rather that we rank-order them (for instance, today I prefer to go to the football game rather than read philosophy).[26]

Even if the critic allows the possibility of intrapersonal comparisons, he may still argue that interpersonal comparisons are not feasible. In other words, we are still unable to assess, on the criterion of the principle of utility, whether I should be permitted to engage in my chosen course of action where it precludes you from engaging in your chosen course. We just cannot say that the pleasure or benefit I receive from free medical care, or from subsidised seats at the opera house, outweighs the pleasure or benefit you receive from paying lower taxes. If such comparisons are not possible, then utilitarianism loses its whole point, since it purports to provide the legislator with a means of resolving such disputes in the right way. In the list of the elements of pleasure and pain, the final element is that of extent – the requirement to take into consideration the interests of all the persons affected by the action in question. This is where we cross the boundary between psychology and ethics. The question now is not how an individual's actions are governed by the sovereign masters of pain and pleasure, but rather what course of action it is right and proper for him to pursue – and, more particularly, to be coerced into pursuing by the sanctions imposed by the legislator. The same sort of calculation that is undertaken by the individual in deciding what course of action to pursue is here undertaken by the legislator, but this time with the added dimension of extent, and thereby taking account of the pains and pleasures of all persons affected by the action. The same rank-ordering will be imposed. The question is more complex than in the case of the individual thinking only of himself – but there is no other methodology, because the calculations in both cases are being done by human beings. So, Bentham's response to the critic can be reconstructed as follows. Given the fact that decisions are being taken, they must be being taken in this way. To say that interpersonal comparisons are impossible is to say that decision making is impossible. The contemporary Benthamite might add that the modern discipline of economics, with its reliance on cost–benefit analysis, is at bottom practical proof that some sort of felicific calculus is not only feasible, but indispensable.

Having said that, the Contingent Valuation Method (CVM) used by modern cost–benefit analysis, which has been soundly criticized by Brian Barry,[27] would probably not have made much sense to Bentham. According to CVM, individuals are asked to state what sum of money they would be willing to pay in order to achieve certain outcomes. The technique is aimed at giving a monetary value to the preference satisfaction of individuals, and by aggregating the results, determining the course of action that would maximize preference satisfaction in the community as a whole. For Bentham, however, the end of action is the maximization of pleasure, and not the maximization of preference satisfaction. It may be true that satisfying an individual's preferences will in many instances maximize his pleasure, but not always – the child who puts his hand in the flame satisfies his preference, but does not maximize his pleasure. CVM would not, in Bentham's view, be equivalent to the principle of utility.

CRITICISM OF BENTHAM'S ETHICAL THEORY

Once we move to the question of extent, we have, as noted above, crossed the boundary from psychology to ethics. Indeed, it is worth noting that many philosophers who are sympathetic to utilitarianism reject the psychological hedonism advanced by Bentham. They accept the criticism that hedonism does not provide a satisfactory account of human motivation. However, they see no difficulty in treating utilitarianism as an ethical theory which stands apart from the psychological basis which Bentham gives to it. Utilitarianism is understood as an ethical doctrine which states that the right action is that which maximizes welfare. An action is evaluated according to its consequences, and in terms of the amount of welfare that it produces. The term welfare is used generically in order to embrace different conceptions of 'the good', for instance, pleasure, knowledge, wealth or the satisfaction of preferences. In other words, what is at issue is whether maximization of 'the good' – in whatever way 'the good' comes to be defined – is an appropriate basis for ethics. Of course, for Bentham, it is the maximization of pleasure and the minimization of pain which matter, and they are the only things that do matter. Nevertheless, the standard criticisms of utilitarianism as an ethical theory apply to Bentham's theory just as much as they do to theories which substitute the more vague term 'welfare' to pleasure. What concerns us here is how Bentham might respond to these criticisms.

Perhaps the most well-known objection is the claim that utilitarianism does not, in the language of John Rawls, respect the distinction between persons. This is a variant of the criticism that utilitarianism justifies the oppression of a minority by a majority. This criticism has a long history. It particularly troubled John Stuart Mill, who responded to it in *On Liberty* (1859) through his 'harm principle'. For Bentham, the problem was rather the reverse of that identified by the critics: it was the minority that tended to oppress the majority – a monarch and an aristocracy (the ruling few) who combined to oppress the bulk of the people (the subject many). Nevertheless, the criticism is regarded as decisive by many commentators, and requires a considered response. In *Theory of Justice*, Rawls argues that utilitarianism does not respect the distinction between persons, but rather regards them as repositories for pains and pleasures, or for units of welfare. What counts are not the persons themselves, but the amount of welfare which can be assigned to them. Moreover, since utilitarianism is an aggregative theory, concerned with producing the greatest amount of welfare, it is insensitive to the way in which that welfare is distributed.[28] In other words, as far as a utilitarian is concerned, a state of affairs in which one person enjoys twenty units of welfare, and four people enjoy one unit of welfare (aggregate welfare = 24 utils) is better than a state of affairs in which the same five people enjoy four units of welfare each (aggregate welfare = 20 utils). This does not seem fair or just – it does not treat people as equals. In the former state of affairs, it is the majority who suffer, and the one who benefits, from the inequality. However, the sums can be manipulated to show that utilitarianism can justify the oppression of a minority. For instance, a state of affairs in which four people enjoy five units of welfare, and one person enjoys one unit (aggregate welfare = 21 utils) is better than a state of affairs in which the same five people enjoy four units of welfare each (aggregate welfare = 20 utils). In this example, assume that the reason that the majority enjoy their additional welfare is because they exploit the person who has just one unit of welfare – in other words, the disadvantage to the minority in a community produces benefits for the majority – then utilitarianism seems to imply that such a course of action is morally right. Some vital interest of a minority might be sacrificed for some marginal increase in the welfare of the majority. Critics find it easier to state the case than to give a plausible example, but, the argument goes, we can imagine a scenario in which a severe injustice is suffered by a minority for the sake, say, of some economic advantage to the majority – it might be that it would be of significant economic benefit to the majority if there existed a minority underclass of slaves.[29] This ties in with Rawls's criticism of utilitarianism, in that if each person were treated as a distinct individual, in other words as an end in himself, such a sacrifice would simply be ruled out. The state would guarantee certain basic entitlements to all citizens before its officials could pursue policies which benefited some more than others. Indeed, Rawls puts it more strongly than this, in that he argues that that even after the basic rights are secured, no policy should be pursued by which any person is made any worse off, even if a vast majority would thereby gain some enormous benefit.[30]

How might Bentham respond to these criticisms? He does expressly reject the idea that the interest of 1,000 persons can be sacrificed without further ado to the interest of 1,001. He recognizes that one has to take into account the total amount of pleasure enjoyed, rather than the number of persons benefited. Hence, the more important or vital interests (and thus greater pleasure) of a smaller number will outweigh the less important interests of a greater number.[31] We begin to see here a way in which the criticisms that utilitarianism does not respect the distinction between persons, and that it leads to the oppression of the minority, which appear to be so intimately linked, do in fact come apart. Even if Bentham treats individuals as repositories of pleasure or welfare, as Rawls claims, this does not mean that the interests of a majority will prevail over those of a minority – the marginal interests of a larger number will not outweigh the vital interests of a smaller number.

Let us pause to explore the nature of vital interests. As we will see below, Bentham argues that the principle of utility has four 'sub-ends', namely subsistence, abundance, security and equality. The latter two sub-ends are of particular relevance here. Security, as we have seen,[32] consists in security for person, property, reputation and condition in life. It is the role of law to guarantee security to every member of society, and this it does by the distribution of legal rights and duties. Ill-informed commentators have been known to remark that Bentham is 'against rights'. What Bentham is against is the idea of natural rights.[33] What he is for is the protection of the vital interests of each and every person – after all, 'Every individual in the country tells for one; no individual for more than one'[34] – and so it will require a very significant benefit for the many in order to justify the sacrifice of the vital interests of the few. It remains true that Bentham's utilitarianism rules out nothing *a priori*. But Bentham sees this as a strength of his position, not as a weakness. There are certain situations in which it is conceivable that the interests of the few should be sacrificed to the interests of the many. After he became a political radical, Bentham was prepared to see the rights and privileges of the monarch and aristocracy sacrificed for the welfare of the people. In fact, without some form of sacrifice of vested interests, no reform programme would ever get off the ground. Yet even then, Bentham was very concerned that existing expectations, even if detrimental to the community as a whole, should be protected. When he proposed the suppression of useless government offices – the sinecures characteristic of eighteenth-century British government – he also proposed that existing officeholders, and even those who had been promised the offices in reversion, should continue to receive an equivalent salary or pension for their lifetime.[35]

Related to the criticism that utilitarianism does not distinguish between persons is the criticism that it does not respect the integrity of persons.[36] Each person has their own unique commitments, responsibilities and projects. Utilitarianism ignores this aspect of what it means to be human, say the critics, but rather treats each individual as an element in a large, impersonal calculation. To take an oft-cited example. A friend of yours is ill and has been admitted to hospital. Your friend is a very popular person, with an extended and caring family, who, you know, will be constantly at his bedside and give him all the support he needs in order to make a speedy recovery. Nevertheless, his friendship is important to you, so you visit your friend, taking a card and a gift of flowers. You get only a brief opportunity to speak with your friend, as he is surrounded by his family and other friends, who have also brought cards and gifts. Nevertheless, you have affirmed your commitment to your friend, even though your visit has only had a marginal impact on his welfare. Now the utilitarian, it is claimed, will argue that, while your action is not wrong, you could have done something much better with your time and resources. In the next ward to your friend is a sick, lonely old man, with no family and friends, and so no one to visit him. How he would have loved some attention – a person with whom to talk and to share his concerns – even from a stranger such as yourself! From the utilitarian perspective, you would have done much better to visit this old man rather than your friend. This, say the critics, reveals what is wrong with utilitarianism. You may think, in contrast, that it shows what is right about utilitarianism. It is curious that critics deride Bentham's utilitarianism because, as we saw above, it is egotistical, and, as we see here, because it is altruistic.

A criticism levelled at utilitarianism by Bernard Williams is that the theory does not have enough ideas. It is too simplistic to capture the depth and complexity of our moral reasoning. This was a criticism which Williams made in an Open University television programme broadcast repeatedly in the 1980s, and which appears in print in a debate with the utilitarian scholar J. J. C. Smart.[37] An obvious response to Williams is merely to point to the projected 68 volumes which will constitute the new edition of *The Collected Works of Jeremy Bentham*, or the 33 large volumes which now constitute the authoritative edition of *The Collected Works of John Stuart Mill*. Bentham and Mill do not seem to have been lacking in ideas if the extent of their output is anything to go by. But an even more satisfactory response is to point to the four sub-ends of utility which Bentham identifies. In fact, many of Bentham's arguments relate directly to the four sub-ends, and indirectly to the principle of utility. Had Williams looked into Bentham's thought in more detail, he would have found a wealth of ideas at this secondary level. It should be recalled that the task of the utilitarian legislator is to introduce measures which will increase the overall happiness (understood in terms of a balance of pleasure over pain), or, more typically, which will prevent a decrease in happiness, using, where appropriate, sanctions (punishments and rewards), themselves composed of pain and pleasure, to discourage actions which are detrimental to the happiness of the community, and (to a lesser extent) to encourage those which are beneficial. This task is undertaken by promoting the four sub-ends of utility – namely subsistence, abundance, security and equality. More specifically, it is the task of the civil law to distribute rights and duties in such a way as to promote these four sub-ends.[38] Security, as we have seen, consists in the protection of the vital interests of the individual – his person, property, reputation and condition in life – which constitute a major component of his well-being. Security is closely related to the notion of expectations, for it involves both the present possession and the future expectation of possessing one's property or other element of well-being. Without security, and thus the confidence to project oneself and one's plans into the future, there can be no civilized life. In short, security is a product of law, resulting from the imposition of rules on conduct.

Subsistence represents the minimum amount of resources which a person needs to survive, and consists primarily in the provision of food, clothing and shelter. Abundance consists in material resources over and above what is needed for survival. Security is connected with the notions of subsistence and abundance. For instance, without the security provided by law, no one will have an incentive to labour, and, therefore, to create wealth (abundance). Moreover, abundance itself is a security for subsistence, since the more wealth a community possesses, the greater the ability to redistribute that wealth to those in danger of perishing from starvation. Indeed, it is subsistence which has a prior claim on all resources in that an individual can be happy only if he is alive. Once wealth has been created, the principle of equality – in essence what today is termed the principle of diminishing marginal utility – demands that it be distributed equally. Bentham argues that, if subsistence requires £100 per annum, the most important £100 which an individual can possess is the first £100. Thereafter, each increment of £100 is worth something less than the previous increment. To put this another way, £100 given to an individual who has nothing constitutes the difference between life and death, whereas £100 given to a billionaire makes virtually no difference at all. Bentham does not, however, advocate the levelling of property, for two reasons. First, if everyone begins at 9.00 a.m. with the same amount of property, by 5.00 p.m. on the same day the intervening deals and exchanges will see inequality re-established – some people will have done better than others. Second, the levelling of property will be an attack on security. Indeed, security, with its attendant expectations, is so important, that it is only in exceptional circumstances, such as providing subsistence to those who might otherwise starve to death, that it is legitimate to redistribute resources, and even here Bentham partly justifies the redistribution on the grounds of security, in that such redistribution will render the remaining property of the rich less liable to violent invasion by the poor.[39]

In relation to abundance, or the creation of wealth, Bentham's basic principle is that of economic freedom. Each individual is most likely to be the best judge of his own interest, since he is most likely to be best informed about his own peculiar circumstances, and most likely to be motivated to act on that information in order to maximize his wealth, and thence his happiness. In a large number of areas in which government had traditionally intervened in economic matters, its intervention was counter-productive. Trade bounties, prohibitions, monopolies and encouragements to population growth belonged to what Bentham termed the 'non-agenda' (although there might always be exceptions). Taking his lead from Adam Smith, Bentham argued that since trade was limited by capital, government could not favour one branch of trade unless it discouraged another branch, since the capital applied to the former had to be taken from the latter. In general, government was best advised not to interfere with the economy, and this included interference in the form of taxation. The imposition of taxation was a form of coercion, and all coercion was an evil in itself.[40] As Bentham remarked: 'The best use that government can make of money in the hands of the lawful possessors is: to leave it where it is.'[41] This is the briefest of outlines of the ideas which Bentham generates from the four sub-ends of the principle of utility, but should be enough to raise some doubts concerning Williams' criticism.

UTILITARIANISM VERSUS INTUITIONISM

Much of the debate concerning the adequacy of utilitarianism as a moral theory revolves around the question as to whether it offers a plausible account of our moral intuitions. For instance, our moral intuition is that we should keep our promises – in making a promise we have made a commitment which we should honour. Bentham, on the other hand, tells us that we should only keep our promises insofar as doing so will promote utility. To broaden this, a utilitarian might argue that we should only maintain the rights which individuals have been granted in so far as doing so will promote utility.[42] This approach is termed 'act utilitarianism', in that one judges each and every act by an appeal to the principle of utility. Some utilitarians, aware of the criticism that this opens the door to abuse and oppression, since certain rights should be treated as fundamental (sacred) and absolute (as Rawls recommends), have developed a version of utilitarianism known as 'rule utilitarianism'. Instead of judging each particular action by the criterion of the principle of utility, it is judged according to that set of rules which maximizes utility. Hence, if the rule which states that promises are always binding, or that rights should always be observed, is better overall (i.e. is utility maximizing) than one which states that promises are not always binding, or that rights are not 'sacrosanct', then the former rule should be introduced and action evaluated accordingly. If the rule which states that persons should not be subject to torture by the officials of the state is better than one that permits such torture, then such a rule should be introduced. Hence, a moral claim on the part of the individual to be protected absolutely in the exercise of certain rights is seen to be compatible with utilitarianism. In other words, utilitarianism is adapted in order more closely to reflect our intuitions. This move, and I cannot emphasize this enough, completely misses the point of Bentham's utilitarianism. This whole approach begs the question. The question at issue is not whether the principle of utility can be so manipulated that its injunctions match sufficiently closely with our intuitions in order to provide a plausible justification for them, but whether the proper criterion of morals is the principle of utility or our intuitions.

An instructive example of the begging of the question is provided by Will Kymlicka in his *Contemporary Political Philosophy*. He takes it for granted that the proper aim of any standard of morality is the treating of individuals as equals. This does not mean equal treatment, since that can give rise to significant inequalities, in that the needs of some individuals, through no fault of their own, are much greater than those of others. The viewpoint he espouses is that of liberal egalitarianism. He then structures his discussion around the question as to which moral theory best promotes liberal egalitarianism. One of the moral theories he considers is utilitarianism, and although he admits it offers an attractive account of equality in some respects, he dismisses it in favour of the theories associated with John Rawls and Ronald Dworkin, who explicitly set out with the aim of promoting equality.[43] You can see how this begs the question. The question at issue is not, as Kymlicka assumes, what theory offers the best conception of liberal egalitarianism, but what is the proper standard of right and wrong. In other words, does utilitarianism or liberal egalitarianism, or some other theory, represent the proper standard of right and wrong? The principle of utility gives significant weight to equality, as we have seen, but Bentham, for instance, argues that for the legislator to aim at equality as his primary end would be both unfeasible and disastrous. The question, to reiterate the point, is not whether utilitarianism offers the best account of egalitarianism, but whether utilitarianism or egalitarianism offers the best account of morals.

For Bentham, intuitionism is one of the main rivals to the principle of utility. It is one variant of the principle of sympathy and antipathy. An adherent of this principle states that the question of right and wrong should be decided by an appeal to his conscience or to his feelings.[44] The modern equivalent of the thinkers whom Bentham criticized are philosophers such as Rawls and Dworkin, who, ultimately, appeal to intuitions as the standard of right and wrong, albeit modified by the introduction of more general moral principles which are intended to structure our intuitions and iron out any inconsistencies. The principle of utility, in contrast, as an 'external' standard[45] gives no weight whatsoever to any existing intuitions as such (though it would recognize the pain of disappointment which accompanies the non-fulfilment of expectations, no matter how unreasonable in themselves). Rather its role is to test and criticize those intuitions, and where they are found wanting, to suggest appropriate alternatives – in other words to determine what is required in order to promote the greatest happiness of the greatest number. If the principle of utility and our intuitions come into conflict, it is not the principle of utility which should be modified, but the intuitions which should be jettisoned. The principle of utility provides a thoroughly critical moral standpoint, and if you do not like its conclusions, then you are adopting the standpoint of the adherent of the principle of sympathy and antipathy. Egalitarianism, in the guise of Rawls and Dworkin, grounds itself on intuitions, whereas utilitarianism, in the guise of Bentham, grounds itself on the sensations of pleasure and pain. Such is the choice.

CHAPTER FOUR

PANOPTICON

THE PROJECTOR OF PANOPTICON

Bentham's panopticon prison has been one of the most controversial aspects of his thought. It has been castigated by libertarians as an affront to human dignity, and the whole of Bentham's utilitarianism tarred with the same brush.[1] A much more dispassionate, albeit still condemnatory, approach has been adopted by Michel Foucault, who argues that 'panopticism' is the characteristic feature of the modern state. He gives the panopticon prison a central place in his account of the transition from the early modern monarchy to the late modern capitalist state. In the former, power is visibly exerted, for instance, by the destruction of the body of the criminal, while in the latter power becomes invisible and focuses on the mind of the subject, in order to identify, marginalize, and 'treat' those who are regarded as incapable of participating in, or unwilling to submit to, the disciplines of production.[2] All this would have seemed very odd to Bentham, who regarded his panopticon prison scheme as humane, and an enormous improvement on the practices of the criminal justice system of the time. This, however, would be to miss Foucault's point. Foucault is not worried at all about the intentions of Bentham as the author of panopticon, and in fact you would hardly guess from his account that the panopticon prison was never built, that standard prison architecture went in a very different direction from that advocated by Bentham, and that Bentham himself did not regard the panopticon as a model for the state (though he did adopt certain principles in his mature constitutional theory which he had first developed for panopticon). What concerns Foucault is to understand the nature of the modern state. What concerns us is to explain Bentham's interest in panoptic architecture, and why he thought it would be such an effective tool in the management of a whole range of institutions.

In the 1790s, having been repelled by the excesses of the French Revolution, Bentham turned his attention to solving two major problems that faced the British state: the first was what to do with convicted criminals; the second was what to do about the poor laws. The initial problem that he addressed, and which chimed with work he had been doing since the 1770s on his projected penal code, and more particularly with his theory of punishment, was that of the criminals. The so-called Bloody Code, whereby hundreds of offences, many of them minor, were subjected to capital punishment, was beginning to meet with increasing opposition. Moreover, the interruption to transportation caused by American independence concentrated minds on the need for the prison – or, as the institution was more commonly referred to, the penitentiary – as an alternative. Transportation had resumed when convicts were first sent to Botany Bay in New South Wales in 1787, but prisons were on, and remained on, the political agenda. Bentham's solution was a building based on the central inspection principle:

> *Morals reformed – health preserved – industry invigorated – instruction diffused – public burthens lightened – Economy seated, as it were, upon a rock – the gordian knot of the Poor Laws not cut, but untied – all by a simple idea in Architecture!* . . . A new mode of obtaining power of mind over mind, in a quantity hitherto without example: and that, to a degree equally without example, secured by whoever chooses to have it so, against abuse.[3]

These were the benefits that would be obtained by the panopticon, or so Bentham claimed at the opening of *Panopticon: or, the Inspection House*, published in 1791. Bentham had initially composed a series of panopticon 'Letters' in 1786, in response to a proposal to establish a new penitentiary in Ireland. The 'Letters' had later been supplemented by two 'Postscripts', which together were about four times as long as the original 'Letters', and in which he elaborated and modified his scheme in several significant respects. The 'Letters' themselves were addressed from 'Crecheff in White Russia'. This was not some sort of strange conceit, because, as we saw in Chapter One,[4] Bentham did actually compose them in the

Crimea. In August 1785 Bentham set out on the greatest adventure of his life. He travelled overland through France to Genoa, from where he sailed to Smyrna. He then boarded an overladen Turkish caique bound for Constantinople. His fellow travellers included a Russian merchant, a surgeon escaping creditors and a slave dealer with a group of African girls. The caique having almost capsized in a violent storm, he managed to transfer to an English vessel for the last part of the journey to the Turkish capital, from where he went overland via Bucharest and eventually joined Samuel at Krichëv in February 1786. Hoping to exploit his skills as a naval architect and engineer, and thereby to make his fortune, Samuel had arrived in Russia in 1780, and had eventually taken up a post with Prince Potemkin, who had put him in charge of his industrial enterprises at Krichëv. As we also saw in Chapter One, the panopticon was not Bentham's original idea – his brother Samuel invented the panopticon. In order to supervise his workforce, Samuel had developed the 'inspection house', where the supervisor, stationed at a central point, could watch over all the activities which were taking place around him. The elder Bentham immediately appreciated the manifold uses to which such a design could be adapted, although it was the prison scheme which circumstances brought to the fore.[5]

THE PANOPTICON LETTERS

I will begin with the scheme as proposed in the initial 'Letters', before turning to the 'Postscripts'. In the 'Letters', Bentham pointed out that the inspection principle was equally applicable to prisons, poor houses, factories, mental asylums, hospitals and schools – anywhere individuals had to be watched or supervised. Ideally, each person should be placed under constant inspection, but failing that, the next best thing was that each person 'should *conceive* himself to be so'. A prison had to achieve a multitude of objectives – safe custody, confinement, solitude, forced labour and education.[6] The beauty of the panoptic architecture lay in the fact that it could achieve them all. The building would be circular, with the cells of the prisoners, divided by partitions, around the circumference, and the inspector's lodge occupying the centre. The cells and the lodge would be separated by an open space, termed the 'annular area'. Each cell would have a window on the outside, and an iron grating near the inside end of the partition, thereby preventing the prisoner from seeing into any other cell. Each cell would be provided with running water and a toilet, while a system of flues would provide heat in cold weather. The inspector's lodge, with its own set of windows corresponding to those of the cells, would be lit by the daylight from the cell windows. An elaborate arrangement of blinds and internal partitions would enable the inspector to see into all the cells, but none of the prisoners would be able to see into, far less through, the inspector's lodge. At night, lamps attached to the outside of the inspector's lodge would throw light into the cells. The inspector would be able to communicate privately with each prisoner by means of 'conversation tubes' – lengths of metal piping specially designed to carry sound – which would run from the lodge to each cell.[7] The inspector would live in the central lodge, as would his family, who would act as informal inspectors. The time they would have spent looking idly out of the window into the street, had they lived in a typical town house, noted Bentham, would now be spent much more productively in observing the behaviour of the prisoners. Moreover, the inspection would extend to the prison officers, who would not be able to commit any abuse without being detected by the inspector. The whole prison would be open not only to magistrates, who would be appointed as visitors, but also to the general public – 'the great *open committee* of the tribunal of the world' – who would ensure that no abuse could be perpetrated by the inspector.[8]

The constant scrutiny of prisoners meant that escape would be impossible, and hence the objective of safe custody would be achieved. And because the prisoners would not even try to escape, realizing that the very attempt would be futile, they would not need to be kept in irons, as traditionally they were in English prisons. Leniency was thereby combined with coercion.[9] The panopticon would also achieve two further objectives of punishment – reformation and economy. Accepting the commonly held view that solitary confinement brought about reformation by forcing the criminal to reflect on his sins, Bentham boasted that, in panopticon, solitary confinement would be perfect.[10] Economy would be secured by the plan of management, which would be by contract. The governor (Bentham referred to the chief officer of the prison as either the inspector, governor or contractor, depending upon the role he wished to highlight) would be granted the right to run the prison for life, subject to good behaviour. In return he would be obliged to publish full accounts of the management of the prison, which, in case of failure, would point the way to future improvements, and in case of success, provide the basis for others to emulate.[11] The prisoners would be forced to labour in any trade which the governor chose for them. Hence, the reformation of the prisoner would be combined with the generation of a profit from his labour. Indeed, reformation and labour were so intimately linked in Bentham's mind, that the latter would provide a measure of the former: 'I know of no test of reformation so plain or so sure as the improved quantity and value of their work.'[12] The governor would not be permitted either to starve or to inflict corporal punishment upon the prisoners in order to make them labour, and he would be financially disadvantaged by every prisoner who died in his custody.[13] The prisoner would have an incentive to labour in that he would receive wages based upon the profit extracted from his labour, which he could use to improve his diet or buy such other items as he desired.[14] The prisoner would also be entitled to a lump sum upon discharge from the prison, related to the profit of his labour.[15] Another advantage to the prisoner would be that he would have an effective security for his health – the governor, living in the centre of the prison, would have an interest in ensuring that it remained free from disease,[16] unlike the typical English prison of the time, where jail fever was rampant.[17]

THE PANOPTICON POSTSCRIPTS

Such was Bentham's plan as conceived in the Crimea in late 1786. Having returned to England, and having been rejoined by his brother, Bentham developed his ideas in the two 'Postscripts'. In relation to the building, Bentham employed an architect, Willey Reveley, to produce a much more detailed plan. The building would be larger, composed of six storeys instead of the four originally projected, and, instead of being round, would be a polygon of twenty-four sides, each side corresponding to the outer width of a single cell. It would be built of iron instead of stone. A permanent chapel (as Bentham remarked, '[t]he necessity of a chapel to a penitentiary-house, is a point rather to be assumed than argued')[18] would be included within the central area, taking over the space which had previously been intended for the top two floors of the inspector's lodge. Five of the cell-widths would become the 'dead-part', forming the accommodation for the governor, his family and staff (they would no longer live in the centre of the prison), and on the outside would form the entrance to the building.[19] Bentham now rejected the principle of solitary confinement, believing that it was more likely to lead to madness than to reformation. His new principle of 'mitigated seclusion' produced some important modifications in the design of the building. The cells would be twice as large as those in the original, accommodating usually two but possibly up to four prisoners – the individuals being grouped together on the basis of their 'age, temper, character, talents, and capabilities'.[20] Apart from saving the sanity of the prisoners, the larger cells would bring financial advantages: first, construction costs would be lower, since half the number of partition walls and toilets would be saved; second, the space would be more flexible in that manufacturing equipment which was too bulky for a single cell might be accommodated in a double cell; third, the choice of employments would be increased, in that tasks requiring the cooperation of more than one worker could be undertaken; and fourth, productivity would be increased, both because an experienced workman could take a boy as an apprentice, and because of the improvement in the 'spirits' – or, as we would say today, in the motivation – of two people working together compared with the same two persons working in solitude.[21]

Bentham had come to realize that there were serious problems with his original plan in terms of rendering the inspector invisible to the prisoners. If the inspector's lodge was dark enough to enable him to see into the cells, it would not be light enough for him to perform the administrative tasks he needed to undertake in order to manage the prison; if the lodge were light enough for him to perform these tasks, he would be visible from the cells. Moreover, if the lodge were divided into sections by screens, when the inspector was in one of the sections, he would not be able to see into the cells corresponding to the other sections. Reveley's solution was to place three annular galleries around the inspection tower, each positioned so that an inspector could see into two floors of corresponding cells, while a series of blinds would ensure that the prisoners could not see into the galleries. The scheme would now require three officers acting as inspectors, each of whom would move around his gallery, taking with him a portable desk or chair at which he would work.[22]

The inspector's lodge, now confined to the ground floor, would be the 'nerve centre' of the panopticon, linked by conversation tubes, not as before to every cell, but to strategic points in the inspection galleries. The inspector could speak directly with his officers in the galleries, who could then instruct a particular prisoner to come to the edge of his cell, from where he could be addressed by the inspector, using a speaking-trumpet. (As is often the case with Bentham's schemes, modern technology would have made them much easier to implement.) The problem of lighting the lodge would be solved by placing a skylight in the roof of the building, thereby allowing daylight to flood into the 'central aperture'. The lodge would contain an open-plan office, divided by movable screens, and a common room, where meals would be taken. The officers would include a sub-governor, chaplain, surgeon and schoolmaster. Any abuse contemplated by a particular officer, or even by the governor himself, would be checked by the presence of the other officers: 'Monarchy, with responsibility and publicity for its checks: such is the best, or rather the only tolerable form of government for such an empire.'[23] It was an 'empire' in which there would be complete and total discipline:

> Here may be observed the first opening of that scene of clock-work regularity, which it would be so easy to establish in so compact a microcosm. Certainty, promptitude, and uniformity, are qualities that may here be displayed in the extreme. Action scarcely follows thought, quicker than execution might here be made to follow upon command.

But how would such discipline be maintained? To the objection that the prisoners would work out when the inspector was not looking, begin by committing minor transgressions, and move on to more serious ones, Bentham responded:

> I will single out one of the most untoward of the prisoners. I will keep an unintermitted watch upon him. I will watch until I observe a transgression. I will minute it down. I will wait for another: I will note that down too. I will lie by for a whole day: he shall do as he pleases that day, so long as he does not venture at something too serious to be endured. The next day I produce the list to him. – *You thought yourself undiscovered: you abused my indulgence: see how you were mistaken. Another time, you may have rope for two days, ten days: the longer it is, the heavier it will fall upon you. Learn from this, all of you, that in this house transgression never can be safe.* Will the policy be cruel? – No; it will be kind: it will prevent transgressing; it will save punishing.[24]

The beauty of the scheme was that it would produce self-discipline.

In relation to the principles of management, Bentham recognized that there were 'few subjects on which opinion is more under the sway of powers that are out of the reach of reason' than that of 'penitentiary discipline'. Some wanted the regime to be severe, others wanted it to be indulgent:

> Some forget that a convict in prison is a sensitive being; others, that he is put there for punishment. Some grudge him every gleam of comfort or alleviation of misery of which his situation is susceptible: to others, every little privation, every little unpleasant feeling, every unaccustomed circumstance, every necessary point of coercive discipline, presents matter for a charge of inhumanity.[25]

Bentham's principles of management, while achieving the ends of punishment, namely, deterrence and reformation, would avoid the two extremes of 'severity' on the one side and 'lenity and indulgence' on the other, and do this at the least possible cost. Hence, Bentham put forward the rules of lenity, severity and economy. By the rule of lenity, the prisoner would not be subjected to corporal punishment or his health endangered. By the rule of severity, the condition of the prisoner would not 'be made more eligible than that of the poorest class of subjects in a state of innocence and liberty' (a principle that he later adopted for his industry-house panopticon, as we shall see). And by the rule of economy, everything would be done to minimize the expense to the public (or, as we would say, the state). The way in which the three rules would operate is illustrated in the diet of the prisoners. Each prisoner would be given as much food as he wanted (as well, it might be noted, warmth during cold weather and care when sick), but the food would be the cheapest available: 'Every man will be satisfied: no man will be feasted, no man will be starved.' The rule of severity would not be violated by the unlimited supply of food, since the prisoner would have no advantage over the innocent poor, who enjoyed 'the liberty of choosing' their food. The rule of lenity would not be violated by the economy because no physical suffering would be produced. And as far as economy was concerned, a well-fed labourer worked better than an ill-fed one.

For Bentham, the rule of economy was the key feature of pan-opticon: 'its absolute importance is great – its relative importance still greater. The very existence of the system – the chance, I should say, which the system has for existence, depends upon it.' The pan-opticon had to be financially viable, and the one source of profit which it commanded was the labour of the prisoners. That profit would be diminished by every unnecessary expense.[26] The key to economy lay in contract management, which produced the junction of the duty and interest of the contractor. The contractor would be motivated by 'the principles of reward and punishment', for what-ever he gained in profit would be his reward, and whatever loss he suffered would be his punishment. While the 'uninterested trustee' (for instance, an unpaid volunteer sitting on a board of governors) might be motivated by love of power, love of novelty, love of reputa-tion, public spirit or benevolence, so might the contractor – but the contractor would also be motivated by something more powerful than any of these, or at least something far more reliable, namely, love of money. The contractor's reward would reflect the success of his management – the more successful, the more money he would make – duty and interest would be joined.[27]

The success of panopticon would depend, as we have seen, upon the profitability of the prisoners' labour. The contractor would choose the trades he considered to be most lucrative, while ensur-ing that the prisoners performed each day a mixture of sedentary and laborious employments. This would maintain the health of the prisoners, but also maximize the quantity of labour each could per-form. The prisoners would have to eat and sleep, but for the major-ity of their time they would be labouring.[28] The prisoners would not, as was customary, be given 'hard labour' as a punishment. Their punishment consisted in the 'coarse diet' and the loss of lib-erty. Bentham's purpose was to teach his prisoners

> to love labour, instead of being taught to loathe it. Occupation, instead of the prisoner's scourge, should be called and should be made as much as possible, a cordial to him. . . . [I]ndustry is a blessing: why paint it as a curse?

Industry was, after all, 'the parent of wealth and population'. The prisoner should be brought to see 'forced idleness' as his bane.[29]

Bentham went into great detail regarding the regimen of the prisoners, including their clothing, mealtimes, hours of work, sleeping arrangements, washing, exercise and education.[30] At the end of his sentence, a prisoner would be discharged only if he agreed to enter the army or navy, or if he found a householder who would be bound for the sum, Bentham suggested, of £50 for his good behaviour (£50 was above twice the annual wage of an agricultural labourer). Otherwise, he would be placed in a 'subsidiary establishment', another panopticon, most beneficially undertaken, suggested Bentham, by the contractor of the prison. The contractor and the 'remanent', as Bentham termed the prisoner who had come to the end of his sentence, would agree on terms, whereby the remanent would labour in the subsidiary establishment for a certain period of time.[31] Bentham was confident that the panopticon discipline would result, in the vast majority of cases, in the 'inward reformation' of the prisoner. He speculated that the prisoner, having received a 'good character' on account of his behaviour in the panopticon, would not find it difficult to find a bondsman, whether a relative, friend or potential employer. If not, he would enter the subsidiary establishment, where his working hours would be reduced, he would be given a curtain to draw across his cell during the times of recreation and sleep, enjoy liberty on Sundays, and be permitted to marry. Rather than being regarded as 'a state of confinement sweetened by indulgences', it should be seen as 'a state of free service, only somewhat better guarded than ordinary against misbehaviour and abuse'.[32]

THE PAUPER PANOPTICONS

While engaged in the attempt to find a suitable site to build his panopticon prison, Bentham became embroiled in the debate produced by the crisis in the administration of the poor laws in the winter of 1795–6. The economy was already suffering from the disruption of trade which attended the war against revolutionary France, and the difficulties had been exacerbated by poor harvests in 1794 and 1795. The wages of labourers had been outstripped by the price of bread, leading to an increase in the number of those who needed relief. Provision for the poor was administered locally by single parishes or groups of parishes, working within the framework established by the Poor Law Acts of 1598 and 1601, and financed by the poor rate, assessed upon each rate-paying householder. The level of relief which might be on offer, whether it was provided to people in their own homes (outdoor relief) or through workhouses (indoor relief), and the expense to the local householders, would, in today's jargon, be called a 'postcode lottery'. In the late eighteenth century there was increasing concern at the cost of poor relief, with some commentators, such as Joseph Townsend and Robert Malthus, calling for its abolition. Matters came to a head in the winter of 1795–6, when the leader of the ministry, William Pitt the Younger, was obliged to take time off from conducting the war effort in order to propose a national scheme for the reform of the poor laws. Bentham could not resist entering the fray, and set out with the intention of producing a comprehensive work on the subject. As often happened with Bentham's schemes, his conception, despite the considerable time and effort he devoted to it, proved to be overambitious. Nevertheless, having criticized Pitt's scheme, and having laid down some 'fundamental positions' of his own,[33] he went on in 1797–8 to make proposals which would, in his view, once and for all solve the problem of poor relief on a national scale. In many ways, the industry-house panopticon scheme was developed in much greater detail than the prison panopticon scheme, although it very much drew its inspiration, and many of its basic ideas, from the latter.

The industry-house scheme was more complicated than the prison scheme for a number of reasons, but most obviously because of the nature of the respective populations of the establishments. The inmates of the prison would be convicted criminals sent there by judges and magistrates, whereas the paupers who entered the industry house, and who (with some exceptions such as suspected criminals and beggars) would do so of their own volition, would consist of persons of all ages, come from a wide variety of backgrounds and occupations, and be innocent of any wrongdoing. The convicts would be subjected to an almost identical regime, whereas the variety within the pauper population would require a much greater degree of discrimination. Bentham set out by drawing up a 'Table of Cases Calling for Relief', in which he analysed the various categories of the pauper population. Of course, the first problem was to define what it meant to be a pauper, or more precisely, to be in a state of indigence. It was important, noted Bentham, to appreciate the distinction between poverty and indigence:

> Poverty is the state of everyone who, in order to obtain subsistence, is forced to have recourse to labour.
> Indigence is the state of him who, being destitute of property . . . is at the same time either unable to labour, or unable, even for labour, to procure the supply of which he happens thus to be in want.[34]

Everyone who had to work for a living was in a state of poverty. It was only if you were unable (or unwilling) to work, or if the value of your labour was less than what you needed for subsistence, that you were in a state of indigence. And if you were in a state of indigence, it was either because of 'internal' or 'external' causes. The former group included those with a physical or mental infirmity, the short-term sick, nursing mothers and children. The latter group included those who had lost work, such as those temporarily or seasonally unemployed, and those who were unable to obtain work, such as criminals or those suspected of being criminals, or those who simply could not provide adequate testimonials for their good behaviour. It also included those whom Bentham termed 'past-prosperity hands' or 'decayed-gentility hands', that is, persons who had lost their property, and who would possibly be granted certain 'privileges', such as a more varied diet and a private living space.[35] Some paupers would need permanent or long-term provision, while others would need relief for no more than a matter of weeks, or even days. The key challenge, as it was for the prison, was financial – how to provide relief without adding to, and indeed by eventually reducing, the expense of the poor rates.

Bentham's solution – and this to begin with – was a network of 250 panopticon industry houses, equally distributed throughout England and Wales, and each able to accommodate up to 2,000 paupers – Bentham having calculated that in the first instance he would need the capacity to accommodate nationally a maximum of 500,000 persons. The scheme would be administered by the National Charity Company, a joint-stock company under the control of a central board, which would appoint a governor to supervise each of its industry houses. The main source of funding would be the receipts of the existing poor rates, together with the income derived from the labour of the inmates and the share subscriptions. The advantage to the parishes was that they would be guaranteed against any increase in their poor rates, and promised a reduction once the Company began to make a profit. The Company would be obliged to provide relief to any person admitting himself into one of its industry houses. It would, moreover, have the power to force certain categories of person – including orphaned and abandoned children, beggars, and persons without any visible honest means of livelihood – into an industry house. Such adults would not be permitted to leave until they had discharged, through means of their labour, the expense they had incurred. Such children – and, indeed, any child deposited there by its parents – would become apprentices of the Company, and would remain in the industry house until the age of 21 if they were male, and 19 if female. Bentham reckoned that, due to the increase in number of pauper apprentices, at the end of 21 years, the Company would have a million paupers on its hands, and hence need 500 industry houses.

The critical point was that the Company's financial viability would depend on exploiting the labour of its children. For the first few years of his life, a child would be a drain on the Company's resources, but once he had reached his early teens, the value of his labour would be equivalent to that of an adult, and so over the course of 21 years (assuming he was admitted at birth) his labour would show a net profit. But though the children would be the major source of profit, there was no one who would not be able to contribute in some way or other, even if it was merely rocking the cradles of babies (Bentham designed a device whereby one old person could rock a dozen cradles at once).[36] Another important feature of industry-house economy was a commitment to recycling – in Bentham's terminology the 'save-all' or 'no-waste' principle. No single particle of animal or vegetable refuse would be thrown away, but all would be 'preserved – collected – and employ'd'. It was the very scale of the pauper panopticons which made it possible to avoid waste: 'Mere juxta-position gives a value to many an article which, if dispersed, would possess none, because the wider the dispersion, the greater the time requisite for collection.' Straw, for instance, would first of all be used as stuffing for the beds, and then placed under the latrines. A 'decrepit old man and woman' would hand out a portion of grass, leaves or hay – depending on the season – to each person as they visited 'the Houses of Office'.

Each week the soil would be removed and emptied on the compost heap. Paupers would be sent around the locality to collect the night soil – a resource, Bentham remarked, the value of which was only just beginning to be appreciated.[37]

The network of industry houses, evenly spread throughout England and Wales, would mean that everyone was within easy walking distance of a house. The large size of the houses, each holding up to 2,000 paupers, brought benefits in terms of economy of scale, for instance, in requiring less building and fewer fixtures and fittings, and fewer officials, than a larger number of smaller houses, and in terms of the possibilities for the division of labour among the workforce. The rooms in the pauper panopticon would be much larger than in the prison panopticon, since again this would reduce building costs and facilitate cooperation. A careful policy of separating those considered to be of bad character from the honest and industrious – and the young – would be implemented, and discipline would be achieved through constant inspection, buttressed by the presence of 'Guardian Elders' – old and, therefore, immune to corruption – among the potentially unruly elements, with authority to report any misdeeds directly to the governor and his officers. The building would be polygonal, consisting of 12 sides, with a diameter of 120 feet. The paupers would be accommodated in apartments around the circumference, with the central inspection lodge occupied by the officers. The building would be divided into 12 'divisions' corresponding to each of the 12 sides. One of the divisions would be set aside for the living accommodation of the officers – equivalent to the 'dead-part' of the prison. Each category of pauper would constitute a 'ward'. It was highly unlikely that the wards would correspond with the divisions, noted Bentham, so one ward might occupy one or more divisions, or one division might be occupied by one or more wards. As in the prison scheme, the lodge and the divisions would be separated by an annular area, which would be crossed at various points by connecting staircases. The divisions around the circumference of the building would contain five floors, of which the top one would be a gallery, while the lodge would be divided into four floors, of which the bottom would be a store room, the middle two would be inspection floors, and the top would form either officers' apartments or a chapel. While the paupers would always be subject to the inspection of the officers, the latter could conceal themselves whenever necessary from the paupers. On the other hand, on certain occasions, certain groups of the paupers would be entitled to some privacy by means of blinds which could be drawn across the divisions.[38] The panopticon design would achieve a number of objectives: the promotion of health and comfort (avoidance of excessive heat and excessive cold, bad smells, and noise); the facilitation of industry (the size and lighting of each room would be adapted to the employments which would be undertaken there); discipline (which would depend on the ease of inspection and the proper separation of classes); the ability to receive visitors; safety against fire; provision for divine worship; and economy.

In terms of the management, the central principle was, as in the prison scheme, the junction of duty and interest, hence things would be so arranged that the more profitably each industry house was run, the greater the reward reaped by its governor. There would, moreover, be safeguards against abuse on the part of the officers. For instance, the pay received by the medical officers would be linked to the rate of mortality in the industry house – insofar as the rate of mortality, compared with the rate in existing poor houses, decreased, their pay would increase, and insofar as it increased, their pay would decrease. Hence, the better the rates of survival of mothers and infants, the higher the salaries of the medical curator and female midwife. This would create an incentive for the introduction and dissemination of good practice. Moreover, the fact that the economic value of an infant to the establishment increased as it grew older gave the Company an interest in its survival. The operations of the whole establishment would be completely transparent, thereby rendering management, as in the prison, subject to the moral sanction exercised by public opinion. Such transparency had the added benefit of allowing each establishment to learn about, and then implement, the good practice developed in any of the other establishments (not to mention avoid the bad practice), and to benefit from any suggestions made by the public at large.[39]

Bentham developed a range of elaborate principles to govern the employment of the paupers. Most important in this respect were the 'permanent establishment', consisting in the apprentices, the feeble and the insane. The 'coming-and-going stock' constituted the second part of the establishment. Each pauper, insofar as possible, would be trained in more than one employment, and, as in the prison, for the sake of health, have one laborious and one sedentary employment; they would have an indoor and an outdoor employment; a peacetime and a wartime employment (the paupers would also form a reserve militia); and in the case of the female apprentices, a mixture of family and manufacturing employments. The main purpose of all the employment would be 'self-supply', that is, the supply by the paupers of their own wants. The Company would not, therefore, come into competition with independent manufacturers, but on the other hand would have a secure market for its goods, even if their quality would have rendered them unacceptable in the market at large.[40] The paupers would receive a proportion of the profit of their labour. But the proverbial carrot was accompanied with the proverbial stick. According to the 'earn-first principle', no pauper would be fed until he had completed his share of work. If the pauper refused to work, he would be fed at the end of two days, and the cycle would begin again. The refractory pauper, noted Bentham, would soon 'be tired of it'. Once a person had, through his labour, paid the cost of his relief, he was free to leave.[41]

A crucial aspect of the scheme was the 'home-fare' or 'cheapest-fare' principle: the food, provided it was not detrimental to health, was to be 'of the least *expensive* kind that can any where be found'. The Company would draw up a suggested list of 'rations', which the governor would be able to choose, depending upon the expense at the place and time of year in question. There would be no alcohol, except for medicinal purposes. Experiments might be made with the diet of the apprentices to see whether a vegetarian diet was more beneficial than one consisting of meat and vegetables, and whether it was better to have two or three meals per day. The expense of feeding the paupers was not to be greater than that required by the independent poor for maintaining themselves. It would be inconsistent with justice, general industry and public economy to render 'the condition of those who are maintained at the charge of others more eligible than the condition of those who are maintained at their own charge'.[42] While the *less* eligibility principle, associated with Malthus,[43] was adopted in the New Poor Law of the 1830s – the condition of the poor receiving relief would be made less eligible, or less attractive, than that of the independent poor – the practical result was the same: you would not admit yourself to the workhouse unless you really needed to do so. The approach was succinctly captured by John Stuart Mill in *Principles of Political Economy*, which appeared in 1843:

> But if, consistently with guaranteeing all persons against abso-
> lute want, the condition of those who are supported by legal char-
> ity can be kept considerably less desirable than the condition of
> those who find support for themselves, none but beneficial con-
> sequences can arise from a law which renders it impossible for
> any person, except by his own choice, to die from insufficiency
> of food.[44]

It may give pause for thought to those who criticize Bentham for his inhumanity and praise Mill for his liberalism and liberality that the former was prepared to be less harsh on the pauper than the latter.

The large-scale nature of the Company, and the centralized man-agement coupled with the national spread, would give rise to a number of 'collateral benefits', argued Bentham, which the exist-ing fragmented arrangements could not provide. We have already seen that the recycling of waste was one benefit, but of supreme importance was the provision of employment for any one who pre-sented themselves for relief. Bentham went on to point out that any demand for labour might as well not exist if no one knew about it. The Company would, therefore, set up a system of Employment-Register and Intelligence-Offices, where demands for labour and offers of service would be compiled and then published in the *Employment Gazette*. Bentham believed that this information would promote the smooth operation of the free market by raising 'scanty' and lowering 'exorbitant' wages and by preventing combinations on the part of both employers and employees. The Company would pro-vide further collateral benefits through its Frugality Banks, which would offer financial services of various sorts to the independent poor, such as short-term loans and savings accounts, which could be converted into pensions, and the transfer of funds. The indus-try houses, operating as 'Frugality Inns' and 'Frugal-Conveyance Stages', would allow a poor man to travel around the country, and earn a wage while doing so, if he had insufficient money to pay for his board and lodging at the 'cheap price of the house'. A fur-ther set of collateral benefits were related to health – for instance, the improved nursing which children would receive would decrease the rate of infant mortality, and the provision of medical care to the sick, through the compilation and dissemination of accurate records, would contribute to medical knowledge and thus improve medical practice. Across a whole range of areas related to farming and manufacturing, by the publication of the various experiments undertaken across the network of industry houses, widespread and wide-scale improvements could be expected.

A further collateral benefit would be the extirpation of begging. Under the existing system, people chose to beg rather than go to the parish for relief, which meant, Bentham pointed out, that such individuals preferred begging to being maintained in idleness. It was not very likely that such persons would give up begging in order to receive relief in one of the Company's industry houses, where, instead of being allowed to remain idle, they would be forced to work and would receive the most frugal fare. On the contrary, Bentham predicted that more people would turn to begging once the Company was established. Begging was 'a species of extortion to which the tender-hearted, and they only, are exposed', while every penny given to a beggar was 'a bounty upon idleness', and constituted 'a sort of insult to the hard-working child of industry: by holding him out as a dupe, who toils and torments himself to earn a maintenance inferior to what is earned by canting and grimace'. Beggars were, therefore, to be compelled to come into the industry house, with rewards given for their arrest, the expense of which would have to be paid out of the beggar's own labour. The beggar would be discharged only when he had settled his account and had received an offer of employment from a 'responsible bondsman', and only when he had served a probation period of one year would he be given a 'certificate of full emancipation'. Those with no visible means of support, and who could be assumed to be professional criminals, would also be compelled to come into the house.[45]

PAUPER PANOPTICON ABANDONED

Such, in brief, was the scheme. But Bentham abandoned it. One problem which he found intractable was the provision of sound financial estimates, necessary if he was to convince both government and private investors that the scheme would be profitable. He needed to know the profile of the pauper population, so that he could show how much income his pauper workforce would generate, but there was an almost total lack of reliable data. He believed that he had worked out a plausible figure for the total number of the pauper population – he had divided the aggregate cost of the poor rates as reported to parliament for the years 1783–5 by the average cost of maintaining a pauper, calculated primarily from accounts of 31 parishes given in Sir Frederick Morton Eden's *State of the Poor*, which appeared in 1797, but also from published descriptions of several poor houses around the country. The economies of scale associated with the proposed industry houses, their connection in a national network, and the 'interested' management of the National Charity Company, would, he claimed, drive down the costs. He recognized that a significant proportion of the paupers would require permanent relief, and would be a constant drain on the Company's resources. Another significant proportion would be composed of the 'periodical-stagnation hands' and the 'casual-stagnation hands', those who were temporarily unemployed either because of the seasonal nature of their work or because of an economic downturn respectively. They would, however, be cost-neutral, in that they would reimburse the Company through their labour for the expense they had incurred before leaving the industry house. That left the apprentices – the children – as the main source of profit. From the point of view of making financial projections, the difficulty was that a child's economic status altered significantly over the course of a few years: Bentham reckoned that a child would start to become productive at about 4 years of age, would meet the costs of his maintenance at the age of 8, and thereafter produce a surplus. The problem which defeated Bentham was how to ascertain the age distribution of the pauper apprentices. It should be remembered that once admitted into the establishment, a male child would not be permitted to leave until he was 21, and a female until she was 19. Assuming no deaths, the number of children in an age group (each such group consisting in the children born in a calendar year) would increase each year as new children entered into that cohort. There would be children coming in all the time, but none would leave – except those who died. Bentham needed to know not only the number of children who would make up each age group at the time the Company was instituted and then at each subsequent period of its existence, but also the rate of mortality for each age group (Bentham himself, as we saw in Chapter One,[46] lost five siblings). Otherwise, he could not estimate the profitability of the Company as a whole. The only relevant figures that he could find were based on a 'census' that he had compiled from the 31 parishes in Eden's *State of the Poor*, which contained not only the number of paupers, but their ages. The problem was that Eden's census was not representative of the country as a whole (first, a large proportion of the parishes were in Cumberland, and second, a large proportion of the individual paupers listed lived in Wolverhampton, and happened to be recorded at a time when many of the men had been called away on militia duty, thus artificially increasing the number of pauper children), and different methodologies had been adopted in different parishes for recording the ages of paupers. Reflecting on the figures extracted from his 'census', he realized that the large fall in numbers it revealed between those aged from birth to 1 year and those aged from 1 to 2 years could not be explained by the rate of mortality.[47] Given that the data he needed were not available, he set about trying to get it for himself. He compiled a blank 'Pauper Population Table', which he circulated through Arthur Young's periodical *Annals of Agriculture*, in the hope that enlightened gentlemen around the country would tour their localities and record the numbers and age distribution of the pauper population. It appears that not a single table was returned to him.

A second problem, which Bentham probably realized was a devastating one for his scheme, arose from the (initially anonymous) publication of Robert Malthus's *Essay on the Principle of Population* in 1798. Bentham had assumed that the Company's profit would arise primarily from the labour of the older children. He was happy, therefore, to admit into his industry houses any child presented to him, and even to encourage the increase of children under the care of the Company by encouraging the apprentices to marry. It had been commonly assumed that an increase in population was beneficial to the state, but Malthus refuted this view, showing that population would tend to increase beyond the means of subsistence, and produce starvation, famine and death, until the equilibrium between population and subsistence was restored. It is not known precisely when Bentham became aware of Malthus's 'principle', but given how well read he was, and how up-to-date he kept himself in relation to current affairs in general, it would be surprising if he had not read, or been told about, Malthus's work soon after its publication. With the projected financial basis of the industry-house scheme fatally undermined, Bentham perhaps saw no reason to carry on with it. Having said that, he did have a habit of moving on to a new project before he had finished the old. In the event, he turned to what had become an even more pressing matter than the poor laws, namely, the expected arrival of national bankruptcy, resulting from the unprecedented expense of the war with revolutionary and Napoleonic France.

Bentham's poor law proposals were, in the end, rather more successful than his prison proposals, in that the New Poor Law Amendment Act of 1834 was directly influenced by his ideas. The economic basis for the scheme was provided by the Benthamite economist Nassau Senior, and its effective administrator was Edwin Chadwick, another 'disciple' of Bentham, who had been Bentham's amanuensis from 1830 to 1832. But even Chadwick did not go so far as to advocate the building of panopticons and contract management.

PRISON PANOPTICON ABANDONED

While Bentham voluntarily abandoned the National Charity Company, the panopticon prison was killed off by the ministry. Both before and during his work on the poor law, he had been busy trying to find a site for his projected prison.[48] He had hoped that the Penitentiary Act of 1779 (on which he had commented in *A View of the Hard-Labour Bill*) would give him the authority to build the panopticon prison, but legal objections meant that a new Act of Parliament was necessary. Between October 1793 and February 1794 Bentham drafted a Bill for Parliament to enact. In the event, the government lawyers, dissatisfied with Bentham's Bill, drafted their own measure instead, which became the Penitentiary Act of 1794, and gave the Treasury powers to acquire land and enter into a contract for a profit-making prison. Bentham's quest to find a site in London occupied him for much of the next decade – it was to be a depressing, and ultimately life-changing, experience. The first two sites he attempted to acquire were at Battersea Rise and Hanging Wood, Woolwich. Rebuffed by local landowners in both cases, acting on the NIMBY (Not In My Back Yard) principle, he turned to a piece of marshy, common land at Tothill Fields. The original Act did not give Bentham the appropriate legal powers to acquire common land, and so he set about drafting a new Bill. The government lawyers rejected this Bill, as they had the previous Bill. Bentham drafted another, which, in early 1798, was adjudged to be an enclosure Bill, requiring, therefore, a different and more complex parliamentary procedure. Finally, in December 1798 the Bill was judged to be a Private Bill, and so could not receive the support of administration. He gave up the attempt to acquire Tothill Fields.

In the meantime, Bentham had been called to give evidence before the House of Commons Finance Committee, and had immersed himself in preparations for the hearings. The Finance Committee, helpfully chaired by his stepbrother Charles Abbot, produced its Twenty-Eighth Report in June 1798, in which it supported the panopticon project, and urged the immediate execution of the contract. Having received this encouragement, in 1799 Bentham did at last manage to acquire, with government money, an estate at Millbank. He was worried, however, that the site was too small, and so composed a long memorial to the Treasury asking for more land and money. The Treasury demanded a shorter memorial of one page, which Bentham prepared. This was considered in August 1800, but it was not until March 1801 that Bentham was informed that the Treasury were minded to abandon the panopticon scheme. Then, in July 1801, to add to the confusion, the Treasury proposed that Bentham build a panopticon on a reduced scale – that he should take 500 instead of 2,000 prisoners – as an experiment. Bentham gave vent to his frustrations and outlined his grievances in *Letters to Lord Pelham* (later titled *Panopticon versus New South Wales*) and *A Plea for the Constitution*, which were printed in 1802 and 1803 respectively, but not published until 1812. The former was an attack on the policy of transportation, and the latter argued that the government was acting illegally in establishing and administering its colonies.

Bentham finally received the news he had been dreading in June 1803 – the ministry had decided that panopticon would not be built. It was reflection on the whole panopticon saga that led Bentham to conclude that government was motivated by sinister interest. Rather than promoting the greatest happiness of the greatest number (the general interest), rulers were naturally inclined to promote their own particular or sinister interest. If they were committed to the general interest, why had they not allowed panopticon to be built? As we have seen in Chapter One,[49] Bentham came to advocate political democracy and eventually republican government. He took central inspection and the junction of duty and interest out of the panopticon, so to speak, and applied it to government in general. Instead of the activities of prisoners being open to the gaze of the governor, the activities of government officials would be open to the gaze of the public.[50] And this is where Foucault's account of panopticon seems to miss the point. According to Foucault, panopticon represents the modern state. Foucault's *Surveiller et Punir*, when translated into English, received the title *Discipline and Punish*, rather than *To Survey and To Punish*. This latter translation, as well as being a more literal translation of Foucault's own title, would certainly have captured the essence of the panopticon prison more closely. Yet, as far as 'panopticism' itself is concerned, the memento 'To Survey and To Discipline' would be still better. The irony in the term 'Punishment' is that, for Bentham, the purpose of panopticon – of central inspection – was to obviate the need for punishment (at least beyond the deprivation of liberty). 'The more strictly we are watched, the better we behave', wrote Bentham.[51] In panopticon, we would be watched all the time, and, therefore, we would behave all the time. There would be no need to punish anyone, or, at least, the need to punish would be rare. This brings us to what, as Miran Božovič has pointed out,[52] is part of the genius of Bentham's plan. For Bentham, the key point was not the fact that the inmates of panopticon would be watched all the time, but, as we have seen, that they would be aware that they might be being watched. The inspector saw an infraction. He did not punish immediately, but waited. He saw a second infraction. At some point thereafter, he would confront the perpetrator with his record book. 'See here, your infractions, with the date and time. This is your punishment.' Once a punishment had been administered, and the prisoners saw that, should they misbehave, punishment was certain, they would no longer misbehave. There would no longer be any need for them to be watched. They would be reformed.

Such was 'panopticism'. Bentham's state, however, was what might be termed 'anti-panoptic'. How and why did Bentham come to advocate 'anti-panopticism'? To understand this, we need to turn to his politics. In the 1790s, as we have seen in Chapter One,[53] Bentham had become politically conservative, in the sense of opposing any significant change to the British Constitution. Like the vast majority of his contemporaries in Britain, he had been in turn intrigued, astonished, outraged and frightened by the course of the French Revolution. Bentham blamed its excesses on its democratic principles. Having in 1789 been prepared to advocate some measure of parliamentary reform, by 1792 he had come to regard such schemes as dangerous, and instead devised measures intended to help the British state solve its various social and economic problems, and fortify it in its struggle against revolutionary France: hence his proposed panopticon prison and industry house. Then, in 1803, as we have seen, occurred the event which was to change Bentham's whole outlook – the British government's rejection of the panopticon prison. Bentham was devastated, and began to talk about the bad faith of the ministry. Over the next few years he developed his theory of sinister interest – that rulers were motivated by a desire to promote not the general interest of the community, but their own particular interest. He saw this first of all in the legal profession when studying the law of evidence, the subject to which he turned following the abandonment of the panopticon scheme. By 1809 he had come to the view that sinister interest infected the whole of the British establishment. The solution was 'democratic ascendancy', which meant a radical reform of parliament by the introduction of universal manhood suffrage (subject to a literacy qualification), annual elections, the secret ballot and equal electoral districts. By 1822, when he began work on *Constitutional Code*, he had moved to an even more extreme position – he had become a republican. He had transformed himself from conservative defender of the British state in the 1790s to leader of the new Radical Party in the 1820s. In Bentham's mature constitutional theory, the central inspection tower disappears as artefact and as metaphor. Every place becomes all-seeing. The people, as members of the Public Opinion Tribunal, ensure good behaviour on the part of their rulers through the instrument of publicity. This is given architectural form in *Constitutional Code* in the minister's audience chamber. The minister occupies the central space, but he is exposed to the full view of the public, who occupy the waiting boxes at the periphery of the building. The more strictly the minister is watched, the better he will behave.[54]

CHAPTER FIVE

POLITICAL FALLACIES

WHAT IS A FALLACY?

Following his discovery of sinister interests and his commitment to democracy, marked by the commencement of his writing on the subject of parliamentary reform in the summer of 1809, politics became Bentham's central concern. He realized that the only form of government which would introduce utilitarian reform was a representative democracy, or at least a government characterized by 'democratic ascendancy', because that was the only form of government which had an interest in doing so. The question then arose – how to implement democratic reform in the face of an intransigent monarch and aristocracy? Bentham's main strategy was to educate the public through the provision of information – facts were necessary, not for their own sake, as demanded by Charles Dickens' character Thomas Gradgrind, the schoolmaster in *Hard Times*, but so that the people might gain the requisite knowledge for pursuing their true interests. Facts were necessary, but not sufficient – argument, based on those facts, was also needed. But argument could mislead as well as enlighten. Hence the people needed to be taught the arts of political argument, and in particular how to recognize and counter fallacious arguments employed by politicians whose interests were opposed to their own, and whose purpose was to deceive them.

Bentham devoted a considerable amount of attention to the question of what made an argument fallacious, and in doing so produced the first major, modern work on the subject. Bentham's writings on political fallacies, composed mainly between 1809 and 1811, but on which he worked sporadically until 1821, complemented his larger project on parliamentary reform. He classified and described in detail the false arguments which had been and, he predicted, would be advanced by those opposed to political reform and improvement, and related them to the sinister interests which prompted their proponents to deploy them. Bentham explained the close connection between his work on parliamentary reform and that on political fallacies in a letter to his friend Francis Place:

> While in name it will be *The Book of Fallacies*, in its effect, the work will include a defence of Parliamentary Reform against the most operative of the instruments of attack that are so continually employed against it: and, as Reform, in all other shapes whatsoever, is so compleatly dependent upon reform in the parliamentary shape, the use of the work, if it has any, in relation to parliamentary reform, will be its principal use – and *that* greater than all its other public uses put together.[1]

This close relationship between parliamentary reform and fallacies, as we have seen in Chapter Two,[2] has been obscured by the way in which the material was presented in the two versions of the work published in Bentham's lifetime, namely Dumont's edition of 'Traité des sophismes politiques', which appeared in *Tactique des assemblées législatives* published in 1816, and Peregrine Bingham's edition of *The Book of Fallacies* published in 1824. Both editors aimed to present the work in a more abstract way than Bentham had conceived it, in order to widen its appeal. While incorporating material omitted by Dumont in which Bentham applied his principles to Britain,[3] Bingham followed Dumont in arranging the fallacies under the headings of fallacies of authority, delay and confusion, but adding fallacies of danger. This was, as Bingham himself recognized, to ignore Bentham's original arrangement of the material. Bentham organized his discussion on the basis of the persons who would typically employ the various fallacies in parliament. Hence he divided them into fallacies liable to be employed by the 'Ins' – members and supporters of the ministry – by the 'Outs' – the opposition – and by 'Eithersides'.[4]

Bentham defined a fallacy as

> any argument that is considered as having been employed, or consideration suggested, for the purpose, or with a probability of producing the effect – of deception: of causing some erroneous

opinion or opinions to be entertained by some person or persons to whose minds it is expected [it] will present itself.[5]

He characterized the state of mind in which fallacy was entertained as a state of delusion. A fallacy was not a false opinion as such, but a discourse which caused a false opinion to be believed, or, by means of a false opinion already believed, brought about some mischievous course of action. A fallacy was distinguished in this respect from a 'vulgar error', a phrase coined by Sir Thomas Browne in the seventeenth century,[6] which denoted only the opinion, and not the consequences which it might produce. Hence, to believe that those who lived in old times were, because they lived in those times, wiser or better than those who lived in modern times, was vulgar error; to appeal to that error in order to prevent the reform of a mischievous practice or institution – to say that a practice should be retained because it had originated in old times and was the product of wisdom – was fallacy (the ancestor-worshipper's fallacy, in Bentham's terminology).[7] The purpose of employing a fallacy was either to produce a false belief, or to prevent some action which would have been beneficial to the community, or, put another way, to produce some action which would be detrimental. To give a recent example: the opinion expressed by British Prime Minister Tony Blair in 2002–3 that Iraq possessed weapons of mass destruction, whether or not it was a conscious lie, turned out to be false, and was, therefore, 'vulgar error'. To go on and say that such weapons in the hands of Iraq were a danger to the security of the United Kingdom, and that the invasion of Iraq was necessary, constituted a fallacy. While, for Bentham, a fallacy was a misleading argument, and not a lie as such, it seems that lying or not telling the truth, or the more subtle variant of being economical with the truth, was intimately connected with the use of fallacy.

Political fallacies were a particular class of fallacies which affected decision making in government. By exposing their irrelevance, the characteristic feature of fallacies, and thus destroying their persuasive force, Bentham hoped to facilitate the introduction and continuation of measures of good government.[8] The use of irrelevant arguments afforded a presumption either of the weakness of the arguments, or total absence of relevant arguments, in support of the cause in question. Fallacies were of use only to a bad cause – a good cause had no need of them. A person who employed fallacies either suffered from 'intellectual weakness', or held in contempt those to whom he addressed them. To be persuaded by them indicated 'intellectual weakness', while to pretend to be persuaded by them indicated improbity:

> The practical conclusion is – that in proportion as the acceptance, and thence in proportion as the utterance, of them can be prevented, the understanding of the public will be strengthened, the morals of the public will be purified, and the practice of government meliorated.[9]

A great deal was at stake.

THE SOURCES OF FALLACY

The reason why politicians employed fallacy, noted Bentham, was sinister interest. A sinister interest, as we have seen,[10] was the interest that a person had in promoting his own happiness, or that of some small group of persons, at the expense of the interest of the community as a whole. If sinister interest did not exist, no one would have a motive to employ fallacies. In the ordinary course of things, the private interest of each politician was in opposition to the interest of the community.[11] Each politician, therefore, shared a common interest, and consequently 'a fellow-feeling', with every other politician. An attack on one of them was an attack on all of them – hence each politician who had a share in this collective sinister interest would defend every other confederate's share with as much energy as if it were his own. Fallacy was the only available means of conducting this defence of abuse.[12] Bentham noted that, in his time, the catch-phrases of the defenders of abuse were 'whatever is, is right' and 'everything is as it should be',[13] constituting an appeal to usage, custom and precedent. Good and bad institutions were defended together on the ground of custom, which was set up as the only proper standard, while the principle of utility was represented as dangerous – which indeed, noted Bentham, it was to sinister interest.[14] Of course, we live in different times, and the fear of innovation which so worried Bentham seems to have been replaced by a mania for change – it keeps the management consultants, lawyers, accountants and advertising executives gainfully employed. But it may be that our age has its 'favourite maxims' which are invoked in order to put an end to argument – statements such as 'it is a viola-tion of my human rights' or 'it is in support of the war on terror' or 'it is racist' come to mind. Moreover, the instinct, or rather artifice, of politicians to defend any statement made or action undertaken by one of their own party gives plausibility and contemporary rele-vance to Bentham's insight regarding collective sinister interest. We will return to this theme when discussing the peculiar difficulties faced by the 'outs'.

Sinister interest, noted Bentham, as well as operating directly, operated indirectly, and often more effectively, through the closely related notions of 'interest-begotten prejudice' and 'authority-begotten prejudice'. A prejudice was an opinion which had been 'embraced without sufficient examination: it is a judgement which, being pronounced *before* evidence, is therefore pronounced without evidence'.[15] Elsewhere, Bentham defined a prejudice as an 'erroneous prepossession'.[16] A fallacy was the product of interest-begotten preju-dice when the person who accepted it failed to realize that sinister interest was his motive for doing so (had he understood the motive, the fallacy would have simply been the product of sinister interest).[17] Interest-begotten prejudice was liable to be far more powerful and thence more mischievous than the sinister interest from which it was derived. There was a limit to the number of persons who could share in a sinister interest – if an interest were shared by a majority of persons it would, by definition, be no longer a sinister interest but the general interest. In contrast, there was no limit to the number of persons who might share a prejudice. Moreover, prejudice was often more difficult to overcome than simple sinister interest:

> Those who are engaged to [the] course in question by no other tie than that of sinister interest, may by sinister interest operat-ing in an opposite direction be in a moment engaged in a course directly opposite: whereas when once the mind is engaged in the trammels of prejudice, although it may have had its origin in sinister interest, there is no saying with what pertinacity and for what length of time it may not persevere in that same course: per-severe, in spite of the opposite action of ever so strong a force of interest – of interest in which ever direction operating.

It was often easier to change the allegiance of those motivated by sinister interest than those motivated by prejudice.[18] The behaviour of the rational actor would be altered in response to new sanctions imposed by the legislator, insofar as an action which had previously been beneficial to the actor had now become mischievous. The irrational actor, that is a person holding some prejudice, might well continue in his accustomed course of action whatever the sanction imposed on him by the legislator.

Bentham pointed out that no one could avoid taking facts and opinions on trust – no one had either the time or the expertise fully to consider the grounds for his opinions except in a small number of matters. Individuals had no choice but to adopt the opinion of some other individual or individuals as their own. Yet the opinion of this 'authority' might be fallacious. In this case, the fallacy was the product of authority-begotten prejudice.[19] Bentham believed that the establishment of the Senate in the United States of America was an example of authority-begotten prejudice. Instead of considering the question as to whether to add a second chamber to the legislature from the point of view of the principle of utility, the Americans had looked at other countries, and in particular Britain, seen the existence of two or more chambers, and without further thought added the Senate to the House of Representatives.[20]

Given the need to take opinions on trust, whose authority could best be relied upon? Bentham argued that the key lay in the probity of the person claiming authority. Now, a person who possessed probity was a person who was disposed to act according to the dictates of the principle of utility – in other words, a person not exposed to the temptations of sinister interest. The most common and obvious manifestation of a deficiency in probity was insincerity, that is, an opposition or discrepancy between the opinion a person declared and the opinion he really entertained. The existence of sinister interest, however, might not only produce an insincere declaration of opinion, but also pervert the opinion itself. Sinister interest, therefore, might produce either misrepresentation of opinion or erroneous opinion. As far as the production of erroneous opinion was concerned, the effect of sinister interest would be to exclude relevant information from consideration (this is to be economical with the truth), or lead to insufficient attention being paid to it. But even assuming that the authority did not lack probity, the reliance that could be placed upon his opinions would differ according to the correctness and completeness of the information he possessed, which in turn would depend on the adequacy of his means for collecting it, and the strength of his motives to employ them. From this perspective, professional authority, argued Bentham, was the most trustworthy, followed by authority derived from power (the greater the power, the greater the capacity to obtain relevant information), then authority derived from wealth (again, the greater the wealth, the greater the capacity to obtain information) and finally authority derived from reputation. The wealthy and privileged were more likely to be intellectually inept and lazy, since they lacked any motive to undertake the hard work necessary to acquire the relevant expertise. They received their distinction from their rank and wealth, and, therefore, had no need to acquire it through their own efforts. Despite this, the wealthy and privileged expected others to defer to their opinion, which, just because they were wealthy and privileged, they did:

> Idiosyncrasies apart, a man of *twenty thousand* a-year will accordingly speak with twice the persuasive force of a man of but *ten thousand* a-year: a man who is everlastingly noble, with some number of times the force of one who is but honourable.

Yet, as we have seen, they were of all authorities the least reliable. I am reminded of the endless procession of 'celebrities' who are interviewed on television 'chat shows', and who seem to expect us to be interested in or influenced by their opinions. It was the professional man, who relied on the accuracy of his opinions for his living, who possessed both the motives and means to procure correct information – to obtain the facts on which those opinions were based – indeed it was the possession of the motives that led him to obtain the means. In short, the professional man had an interest in truth.[21]

Appeal to authority was fallacious when substituted to relevant arguments which were within the capacity of the debaters to understand, and more especially so when the authority in question was the opinion – real or pretended – of any person whose interest was opposed to that of the people.[22] To appeal to authority as the proper standard for judging a law or established practice was to accept either that the principle of utility was not the proper standard, or that the practice of earlier times or the opinion of other persons was the proper standard. To accept the former proposition was to acknowledge oneself to be an enemy of the community, and to accept the latter to acknowledge oneself incapable of reasoning.[23] I am reminded of an advertisement for the *Financial Times* which came to its climax with the tag line 'No *FT*, no comment', and hence claimed to be the sole authority in the country. If you did not read the newspaper, you could not have an opinion; if you did have an opinion, it was because you read the newspaper. No one escaped the insult.

Bentham's analysis is all very reassuring from the point of view of the university academic! We might argue that academics are the most legitimate authorities in their respective fields because they have no sinister interest in promoting false opinions, a product in turn of their belonging to an institutional structure which rewards the discovery of truth. At least, that is how things ought to be arranged. Bentham's own paradigm of the professional was the medical practitioner, but the range of persons who call themselves 'professional' has widened significantly since Bentham's time. There are some professionals whose opinion we might want to treat with a certain degree of suspicion. For instance, the views of those medical practitioners and scientists who work for tobacco companies and for the alcoholic drinks industry, and to some degree those who work for pharmaceutical companies, should not be accepted at face value. It is not that they are any less well qualified or less intelligent than the academic, but that they have an interest in promoting products which many people have cause to think produce more harm than good. And who has a greater sinister interest than those ingenious 'professionals' who work for the advertising industry (apart, perhaps, from lawyers)? The advertisers are the persons who make the strongest claim for our trust, yet are almost the last persons to whom we should give it.

The reason why fallacies were accepted by those to whom they were addressed, but against whose interest they operated, argued Bentham, was the existence of intellectual weakness, which consisted of 'ignorance in respect of every thing by which, whether in a beneficial way or a pernicious way', one's interest was affected.[24] For instance, the belief that there existed 'a natural association between aristocratical superiority and virtue' was an error which favoured the sinister interest of the monarch and aristocracy to the detriment of the people in general.[25] For a more prosaic example, let us return to the boy who puts his finger into the flame of the candle, and burns himself. Imagine that his spiteful elder brother had said to him: 'Look how pretty the flame of the candle is! Because it is pretty to look at, it is also nice to touch. Put your finger into it.' The boy had been persuaded by the fallacy, and thereby demonstrated his intellectual weakness. As Bentham remarked, at the root of every 'anti-popular arrangement', there was 'honest intellectual weakness'.[26] If people in general had not suffered from 'intellectual weakness', then the delusion which originated in sinister interest, interest-begotten prejudice and authority-begotten prejudice, would not have been able to establish itself. Whereas the people had an interest in gathering as much information as possible, and of hearing arguments and comments upon it, rulers, in contrast, had an interest in suppressing criticism of both the form of government and of their activities under it, and hence of limiting the freedom of the press through laws of libel and defamation. To deter criticism of government officials in this way was

> to destroy, or proportionably to weaken, that liberty, which, under the name of *the liberty of the press*, operates as a check upon the conduct of the ruling few; and in that character constitutes a controuling power, indispensably necessary to the maintenance of good government.

Bentham did not advocate a free-for-all, but argued that truth should constitute a defence in law. The security for good government resulting from the liberty of the press far outweighed any evil which might be produced in the case of the particular individuals who were the subject of the imputations. Indeed, as far as government was concerned, the more senior the official in question, the greater the resources he could deploy to refute any accusation made against him, while the benefits arising from his office (the exercise of power, for instance) abundantly compensated him for any inconvenience he might suffer.[27]

As we have seen, Bentham stated that the proper object of every political arrangement was the greatest happiness of the greatest number. However, in every political community, with the exception of the representative democracy of the United States of America, he believed that the interest of the many had been sacrificed to the sinister interest of their rulers. Rulers were no different from any one else, in that they were motivated predominantly by their self-regarding interest. This self-regarding interest led them to defend every abuse that they found established, whether or not they derived any profit from it, since the reform of one such abuse might lead on to the reform of others. Permit one abuse to be reformed, the rest would be vulnerable. In parliament, both the 'ins' and the 'outs' (the government and opposition) were motivated by the same sinister interest, and both were prepared to employ whatever fallacies promoted that interest. The situation of the 'outs', however, was slightly more complex. Their object was to force the 'ins' from office, and thereby become the 'ins' themselves, by raising their own political reputation and lowering that of the 'ins'. The 'outs', therefore, attempted to promote that portion of the universal interest which did not conflict with their own sinister interest, and to diminish the reputation of the 'ins' by using fallacies to oppose any beneficial arrangements proposed by the latter. The 'outs' had to balance the advantage to their share in the universal interest from the establishment of a good measure proposed by the 'ins', against the rise in their own reputation in the event of successful opposition. In respect of a bad measure by which the sinister interest of both 'ins' and 'outs' would be promoted, the 'outs' had to decide, if they successfully opposed the measure, whether the loss to their sinister interest would be outweighed by the gain in reputation.[28]

While Bentham's analysis was directed against the Whigs and Tories in the unreformed parliament, some elements of his analysis remain pertinent today. The sort of political manoeuvring which he describes is the staple of party politics. Take, for example, the vote in the House of Commons on the Racial and Religious Hatred Bill on 31 January 2006. The New Labour government's chief whip, Hilary Armstrong, suffered the embarrassment of allowing Prime Minister Blair to leave the House before the vote was taken, and then seeing the government defeated by one vote. According to 'one Labour insider', 'We thought we had a deal with the opposition and we thought we knew what our own MPs would do. Some people who said they'd vote with us voted against or abstained'. David Cameron, the leader of the Conservatives, was, therefore, able to add to his credentials as a plausible prime ministerial candidate by taking credit for what was described as 'the first "classic ambush" which the hitherto hapless Tories have managed in years'.[29] The trick for the opposition is to persuade the public that you are acting for their benefit, while opposing as many measures of government as possible. To inflict a defeat on government in such circumstances increases the reputation of the opposition, and diminishes that of the government.

DELUSION

Bentham recognized that 'deviations' existed between the wishes of the people in general and the measures dictated by the principle of utility. He remained optimistic that the deviations were becoming 'less and less numerous, and less wide', and that eventually 'coincidence will be complete'.[30] Having said that, the promotion of good government would be impossible if the opinions of the people were not in line with its true interests. The fact that this coincidence did not exist meant that the people were suffering from delusion. Individuals, their understandings perverted, adopted 'some erroneous conception or opinion', and were thereby induced to 'give support to misrule: namely adding themselves to the number either of those over whom it is exercised or those by whom it is exercised'. Rulers wished to promote the belief that those who actually possessed the powers of government were also the best persons for exercising those powers, and that the more power, wealth and titles of honour a man possessed, the greater the degree of talent and virtue he possessed.[31] Those delusive beliefs might be produced directly by means of fallacious argument, though they might also be produced indirectly through an association of ideas. For instance, the head-covering called a crown and the chair called a throne were designed to persuade the people that the monarch, who wore the one and sat on the other, was a being of 'superlative excellence'. It was 'to the disgrace and sad affliction of the species' that the head-covering and the chair produced the effect it did:

> Wherever they see the external instruments of felicity heaped upon one object, there [the people] fancy they see excellence: excellence, moral or intellectual, or both together: and on this vitiated state of the people's visual organs is the dependence of their adversaries . . . for the success of the imposture.

Bentham took comfort from the fact that such 'impostures' did not exist in the United States of America, where the people enjoyed much greater happiness than in 'all Monarch-ridden states'.[32]

Delusion, then, was the state of mind produced by fallacy (though delusion might have other causes as well). Sinister interest led rulers and other officials to employ fallacies in order to produce delusion, and thence to promote and defend the abuses from which they profited.

EXAMPLES OF FALLACIES

So much for the sinister interest which led politicians to deploy fallacies, and to produce delusion in the minds of those who accepted their arguments. Now for several examples of particular fallacies, taken from the class of arguments appealing to men's superstitions, and beginning with the ancestor-worshipper's fallacy. (Bentham gave what he considered to be pithy and memorable names to each of the fallacies he identified.) This fallacy, which I briefly alluded to above, consisted 'in a supposed repugnancy between the proposed measure and the opinions of men by whom the same country was inhabited in former times'. These opinions were brought to mind by such phrases as the wisdom of our ancestors, the wisdom of ages, venerable antiquity and the wisdom of old times. In Bentham's view, experience was 'the mother of wisdom', but, according to this fallacy, it was inexperience that produced wisdom. The fallacy was plainly absurd, but gained its plausibility from a misnomer. The portion of time which, in relation to the present, should have been called 'young' was 'dignified with the name of *old*'. Old times, in common speech, referred to times in the past. Now, in relation to individuals, there was good reason to regard seniority as a proper cause of respect, and to regard an older person, who therefore possessed greater experience, as being wiser, all other things being equal, than a younger person. But, said Bentham, compare a man aged 50 living in 1500 to a man aged 50 living in 1800: the man of 1800 would be considered to be wiser than the man of 1500. So past times, in relation to the present, should be termed young times, in that the present times had more experience, and hence more knowledge and wisdom, than past times. And whatever knowledge inhabitants of past times had of their own times or of the times before theirs, they had no knowledge of present times. The people of present times, when informed that a practice could not be changed because it had always been done in that way, were being told to prefer a judgement

grounded on no evidence to a judgement 'grounded on the correct-
est and compleatest that can be obtained'.[33] It was only in ethics and
religion that the wisdom of our ancestors fallacy had influence – we
did not, for instance, rely on the wisdom of our ancestors when it
came to modes of travel, to providing artificial light and heat, to
making clothes, and to 'curing, alleviating or preventing disorder
in our . . . bodies'. The explanation lay in the existence of sinister
interest in the 'leading men' in politics and religion.[34]

A further group of fallacies appealed to men's superstitions.
Two related fallacies which Bentham discussed were the posterity-
chainer's fallacy and the Jephthah's vow-pleader's fallacy, both
of which were variants of the ancestor-worshipper's fallacy. The
object of both fallacies was to restrain future legislators, which, in
Bentham's view, was a mischief in itself. The posterity-chainer's fallacy referred to the case where a contract was entered into either
by two sovereigns, or by a sovereign and his subjects. The purpose,
noted Bentham, was to fix 'an everlasting yoke . . . upon the neck
of all posterity'.[35] It was bad enough being subject to living tyrants,
but to be subject to dead ones was still worse. Those who entered
into such arrangements attempted 'to extend their tyranny over all
future generations'. Bentham posited a situation in which a particular law, which had been pronounced to be immutable, had in fact
produced some good at the time of its enactment. Over time, the
law became detrimental to the general welfare. But the country was
prevented from getting rid of it. A living tyrant might be persuaded
to repeal a mischievous law. A dead tyrant could repeal nothing.[36]
The proper way of proceeding was either to give the law an indefin-
ite duration, so that it remained in force until repealed or amended
by the same authority that had enacted it, or to give the law a def-
inite duration, but again make it liable to be repealed or amended
before that period had expired. This was the principle of 'defeasible
perpetuity'.[37]

Two examples of posterity-chaining laws were the 'immutability clauses' in the French Constitution of 1791 and the Spanish
Constitution of 1812 – no change to the respective constitutions was
permitted for a certain number of years. Another example was the
French Declaration of Rights of 1789, which claimed that the rights
of man it had announced were 'imprescriptible', and still another the
attempt of the English lawyer, Sir Edward Coke, to claim that, to the
end of time, any statute that contradicted the provisions of Magna

Carta would be void.[38] Bentham argued that immutability was of no use to good laws, since good laws would be supported by their utility. The attribute of immutability was of use only to bad laws – the worse the law, the more it needed such support. Indeed, the very attempt to claim immutability for a law should be regarded as a confession of its mischievousness.[39] As Bentham explained (I have updated the illustration), if the conduct of the people of 2009 were to be determined by those of 1909, and those of 2109 by those of 2009, then

> in process of time the power of legislation would become extinct: the conduct and fate of all men would in all points be determined by those to whom their exigencies were unknown: no new exigencies would be capable of being provided for: and the aggregate body of the living would remain for ever in subjection to an inexorable tyranny exercised, as it were, by the aggregate body of the dead.[40]

Bentham concluded that

> the existence of any thing in the shape of law that shall be absolutely immutable will be seen to be radically repugnant with the welfare of every human being, and of every aggregate body of human beings, how small or how large soever.[41]

The Jephthah's vow-pleading fallacy added the ceremony of taking an oath, and thence the guarantee of a supernatural power, to the making of the law or agreement in question. The allusion is to the biblical story of Jephthah, who vowed that, if God brought him victory in battle, he would sacrifice the first thing which came out of his house to meet him on his return. Having destroyed his enemies, he came home and was appalled to find himself greeted by his daughter – his only child. He had, however, made his vow, and so burnt her to death.[42] In order to commit this fallacy, said Bentham, you needed a book which must be called the Holy Gospels, and a man called an Archbishop or Bishop to recite to you, one after the other, the things it suited you to do, whereupon you solemnly promised and swore to do them.[43] Bentham no doubt had in mind George III's claim that the Coronation Oath he had taken on his accession to the throne in 1760 prevented him from giving assent to any measure of Catholic Emancipation, thereby prompting Pitt the Younger to resign as leader of the ministry in 1801. A further absurdity involved in this fallacy, noted Bentham, was the idea that Almighty God could be bound by such a ceremony: it was to claim that God could be bound by a mere human being – by any single one 'of all the worms that crawl about upon the face of this minute speck in the mundane system called the earth'. On the other hand, if God was not bound, the ceremony was worthless. The posterity-chainer claimed power over all successive generations; the Jephthah's vow-pleader not only over all successive generations, but over God as well.[44]

A further device in the category of arguments appealing to men's superstitions was the allegorical-personage-worshipper's fallacy. This fallacy consisted in using, as the name of some organization or group of people, the name of some fictitious or allegorical person to whom it was customary to attach the attribute of excellence. So, instead of rulers, you said 'the Government'; instead of Churchmen, you said 'the Church'; and instead of lawyers, you said 'the Law'. The persons concerned thereby gained more respect than they would have received if called by their proper name.[45]

We might think that in our so-called post-modern age we would be hard pressed to find examples of the posterity-chainer's device. However, Bentham might well have thought that a great deal of our political and legal discourse exemplifies the posterity-chainer's fallacy – namely, every appeal to some declaration or other of human rights, or to some fundamental clause in a constitutional document. It often seems to be assumed that the rights contained in such declarations have existed since time began, or at least have existed since the moment that some (fictional) social contract was entered into, and will remain in force until the end of time.

FALLACIES TODAY?

Do politicians use fallacious arguments of the sort which Bentham identified? Just pick up a newspaper, or listen to the news bulletins, and see if you can pick out an example or two. I should add that I have so far mentioned only a handful of the 30 or more fallacies which Bentham identified, but will allude to several more below.

In October 2005 there was a tiff between the British executive and judiciary in relation to the former's proposed anti-terror legislation, and in particular the proposal to give power to police forces to hold terrorist suspects for 90 days without charge. *The Guardian* of 12 October 2005 reported as follows:

> The government should not attempt to browbeat judges over its new anti-terrorism laws, the new senior judge in England and Wales warned . . . . The lord chief justice, Lord Phillips of Worth Matravers, said judges were not in conflict with the government but said that it would be 'wholly inappropriate' for a politician to try to put pressure on them. . . . Tony Blair denied that he was 'brow-beating' the judiciary and went on to warn the judges – again in explicit terms – that they must not rule against the anti-terror measures that were being proposed. 'When the police say this is what we need to make this country safe, you have got to have good reasons to say no to that.'

This remark of Prime Minister Blair is, on the surface, an example of the appeal-to-authority fallacy, as well as a further example of the allegorical-personage-worshipper's fallacy ('the Police'). One might respond that Blair is making a valid appeal to professional authority, the most reliable form of authority – though one would need to consider whether the judgement of policemen is affected in any way by sinister interest. Blair's appeal to authority, however, appears in a more dubious light in the context of a further report in *The Guardian* of 21 November 2005:

> the much-trumpeted support senior police officers gave [to the clause to hold terrorist suspects for 90 days] does not extend to the entire [anti-terror] bill . . .. The Association of Chief Police Officers [ACPO] privately opposed four of the government's 14 main proposals announced after the July 7 [2005] London bombings.

So, Blair did not merely commit the appeal-to-authority and allegorical-personage-worshipper's fallacies, but also what Bentham termed the lumping-classifier's fallacy. This amounts to taking a more general proposition, which is nothing to the point, in order to justify a more specific proposition. General proposition: ACPO supports the anti-terror legislation in general; specific proposition: criticism of any part of the anti-terror legislation is unjustified. In more familiar language, this is to beg the question.

Now for an example of Prime Minister Blair appealing, in relation to the same measure, to another clutch of fallacies – fallacies addressed to men's fears – and, once again, to the lumping-classifier's fallacy. In Prime Minister's Question Time on 9 November 2005, in response to a question from the Conservative leader Michael Howard calling into question the proposal to allow the police to keep suspected terrorists in custody for up to 90 days without charge, Blair said:

> We are not living in a police state, but we are living in a country that faces a real and serious threat of terrorism – terrorism that wants to destroy our way of life, terrorism that wants to inflict casualties on us without limit – and when those charged with protecting our country provide, as they have, a compelling case for action, I know what my duty is: my duty is to support them, and so is the duty, in my view, of every Member.

This appears to be a variation of the suspicious-character-imputer's argument on the ground of name. The bad name today is not, as it was in Bentham's time, the Jacobin or the anarchist. Today the bad name is the terrorist. The fallacy, according to Bentham, consists in linking the opinions or conduct of the persons in question to certain, other obnoxious persons, but with whom no personal intercourse had taken place, or with whom there was no possibility that any personal intercourse could take place.[46] The proposed anti-terror bill contained a clause banning a group called Hizb ut-Tahrir, who were 'alleged' to be 'extremists', even though ACPO knew of no intelligence to justify such a ban.[47] As for the lumping-classifier's device, as we have seen, you take a more general proposition which is nothing to the purpose in order to justify a more specific proposition. Hence, the existence of a terrorist threat is used to justify the detention of terrorist suspects for up to 90 days; what is missing is a relevant argument which shows why such detention is necessary.

An example of the ancestor-worshipper's fallacy comes in a question asked by a journalist. On BBC Radio 5 Live on the morning of 17 January 2006, Nicky Campbell was interviewing Chief Inspector Gary Gearty of Cleveland Police in relation to initiatives being introduced to deal with prostitution in Middlesbrough. Campbell asked: 'Shouldn't you be concentrating on other areas of crime, rather than prostitution which has been happening since time began?' It may well be a valid question to ask, but not for the reason given. Things have always been like this, therefore they should always continue to be like this; our ancestors have always done this, therefore so should we.

On 11 January 2006, the question of the abolition of primogeniture in relation to the succession of the Crown was raised in the House of Lords. Lord Falconer, the Lord Chancellor, responded:

> My Lords, it is not right to have gender discrimination, including in the choice of the succession, but there is no groundswell for change. A change would require complex constitutional legislation and consultation with the Commonwealth.

Lord Falconer, therefore, used three arguments to reject the proposal: first, that there was no public demand for it; second, that it would prove complicated; and third, that consultation would be necessary. The first argument appears to be the equivalent of Bentham's all-hush-without-doors or nobody-grumbles fallacy. This fallacy consists in the argument that because no one is complaining, there is no need for the proposed remedy. Bentham argued that, just because there was no complaint, it did not mean there was no grievance. To put this in another context: the wily politician, when imposing a tax, would prefer to impose it upon those who would suffer more from having to pay it, providing they were less likely to complain about it than those who could more easily bear it. The criterion is not who can best afford it, but who will complain the least about it.[48] The second and third arguments employ the importance-and-difficulty-trumpeter's fallacy, where phrases such as 'extreme difficulty of the business' and 'need of caution and circumspection' is 'the prattle which the magpye in office . . . deals out among his auditors as a succedaneum to thought'.[49]

Another set of fallacies which are still very much in circulation are personalities-vituperative fallacies. The general thrust of these fallacies, remarked Bentham, was to direct attention to some 'supposed imperfection on the part of the man by whom a measure is supported' in order 'to cause men to impute a correspondent imperfection to the measure'. Variations on this theme were: (1) that the proposer of the measure had a bad design; (2) that he had a bad motive; (3) that he was a person of bad character; (4) that he was inconsistent, in that on a former occasion he had opposed the measure or had said something which appeared to contradict what he said on the present occasion; (5) that he was friendly with another man or group of men who had advocated dangerous principles or designs; (6) that he shared the same name with some person or set of persons who advocated bad principles, or were of a bad character, or had done bad things.[50] The inconsistency argument has been applied on more than one occasion to David Cameron, leader of the Conservatives. *The Metro* carried the following report on 17 February 2006: 'Commons leader Geoff Hoon criticised [David Cameron] for taking the maximum two weeks paternity leave. He said: "We all know he voted against the law when it came before the House."' Geoff Hoon's criticism, of course, is directed not towards the measure, but towards the leader of the opposition. The conclusion which we are asked to draw is that any measure which David Cameron proposes is to be regarded with suspicion on the grounds of his inconsistency in relation to some other measure.

Another example of the personalities-vituperative fallacy can be seen in a letter to *The Guardian* sent by New Labour MP Siôn Simon, published on 13 January 2006. The subject was criticism made by General Michael Rose of Blair's invasion of Iraq in an article published in the same newspaper on 10 January 2006. Simon pointed out that Rose had opposed the Nato bombing of Serb positions during the Milosevic regime, and that such unwillingness to intervene had led, in the opinion of Ian Traynor, *The Guardian's* 'Balkan expert', to the Srebenica massacre of July 1995, when 7,000 Muslim males had perished. Simon concluded: 'The prime minister's record in tackling dictators such as Saddam Hussein and Slobodan Milosevic is perhaps not best questioned by those whose own record of leadership is so authoritatively criticized.' The fact that a man deployed bad arguments in relation to one measure (the criticism here relies on authority, of course), does not in itself mean that his arguments in relation to a different measure are bad.

And again, in November 2005 we had John Prescott, at the time deputy prime minister, referring to Sir Christopher Meyer, who had published memoirs of the period when he served as British ambassador to the United States of America, as a 'red-socked fop', in an attempt to force him from his job as chairman of the Press Complaints Commission.[51] A friend of Sir Christopher might have referred to his sartorial flamboyance. But this would be to commit the personalities-laudative fallacy.

Bentham ranged a further group of fallacies under the general alternative headings of the question-begging-denomination-employer's device, or eulogistic and dyslogistic-appellative-employer's device, or laudatory and vituperative appellation-employer's device. Bentham pointed out that by giving the same thing a different name it was possible to arouse feelings of approval or disapproval. Some names were 'neutral', such as desire or labour. Some, however, had a sentiment of approval attached to them, such as 'industry', and these were 'eulogistic' terms, while others had a sentiment of disapproval attached to them, such as 'lust', and these were 'dyslogistic' terms. Bentham explained the corresponding fallacy as follows. When one referred to the conduct, intention, motive or disposition of some person who was indifferent to you, you employed the neutral term; of some person whom you wished to be well thought of (someone of your own party), you employed the eulogistic term; and of some person whom you wished to subject to aversion or contempt, you used the dyslogistic term. The implication was that the person in question deserved to be praised or blamed.[52] British Prime Minister Gordon Brown, for instance, is often described as 'dour' – an epithet not uncommonly applied to persons from Scotland – with the intention of portraying him in an unflattering light. In contrast, his supporters refer to his 'decency and integrity'.[53] The language you use is conditioned by the side you are on.

CONCLUSION

By exposing the nature of fallacious political argument, Bentham hoped to prevent its use. The more the public was convinced of the insincerity of the politician who advanced such arguments, the greater the restraint imposed on the employment of them. The greater mischief, however, was not the employment of bad arguments, but the acceptance of them as influential or conclusive. It was important not only that politicians were made ashamed to express them, but also that the people in general were made ashamed to accept them. One method of helping to extirpate fallacious argument, suggested Bentham, would be to take a printed report of the debates of the House of Commons, and mark up the fallacies employed.[54] (Bingham and Charles Austin did precisely this in 1826[55] – a similar exercise with debates in today's House of Commons or US Congress might be instructive.) A further practical recommendation which

Bentham made was the installation of a Table of Fallacies into the debating chambers of legislative assemblies. If a speaker presented a fallacious argument, the president of the assembly, who would be supplied with a wand of appropriate length, would point to the fallacy in question on the Table. Perhaps political commentators and journalists, when interviewing politicians on television, should be supplied with a similar device, whereby the name of the fallacy would appear across the top of the screen. The viewer could then press his red button to see an explanation of the fallacy.

It does seem that Bentham has an important message for us, and that some very serious thinking ought to be done in relation to the quality of our public debate. Bentham was optimistic that, as the world grew older and at the same time wiser, 'which it will do unless the period shall have arrived at which experience, the Mother of Wisdom, shall have past child-bearing', the influence of authority, particularly in parliament, would diminish. In private morality, private law and constitutional law, as 'the body of experience has encreased, authority has gradually been set aside, and reasoning, drawn from facts and guided by reference to the end in view, true or false, has taken its place'. It was only in matters of law and religion that efforts were made to obstruct as far as possible the exercise of 'the right of private inquiry'. In every branch of physical art and science, the folly of appealing to authority instead of direct and specific evidence was universally acknowledged. In the moral branch of science, including religion, the folly would likewise be universally recognized were it not for the sinister interest of rulers.[56]

A philosophical issue raised by Bentham's work on political fallacies is the relationship in his thought between truth and utility. It is a long-standing debate in philosophy as to whether it is ever appropriate to tell a lie. Utilitarianism is criticized for not having an absolute commitment to truth: if the benefits of telling a lie, so the argument goes, outweigh the benefits of telling the truth, then the right action, according to the utilitarian doctrine, is to tell a lie. Bentham agreed that it would be absurd, for instance, to give truthful information to someone who would use that information to perpetrate an evil. (Kant's view is that we should always tell the truth – but voluntarily to tell the mad axeman that his intended victim is hiding in the shed at the bottom of your garden does indeed seem an absurd thing to do.) Yet the implication of Bentham's writings on political fallacies is that politicians should never mislead the public, and in his writings on judicial procedure he is clear that the point of such procedure is to discover truth. Moreover, in his writings on logic, he suggests that truth and utility are so linked that to utter a truthful statement is the equivalent of uttering a statement consonant to the principle of utility. If truth is utility, then how do we explain the useful lie? Now that really is a perplexing question – and one that deserves a more thorough investigation than it has received here.

CHAPTER SIX

RELIGION AND SEX

JOHN BOWRING AND THE GROTES

Although born into a staunch Church of England family, by the age of 16, as we have seen in Chapter One,[1] Bentham had become sceptical of religion. The critical moment arrived when, in order to take his degree at the University of Oxford, he was required to subscribe to the Thirty-nine Articles. He could have maintained his intellectual integrity by refusing to do so, but would have gravely disappointed and alienated his father, whose great ambitions for his elder son would have been dashed. He gave way, and subscribed.[2] In the course of his subsequent career, Bentham published three major works on religion. The first, and the only one which appeared under his own name, was *Church-of-Englandism and its Catechism Examined*, printed in 1817 and published the following year. Here Bentham attacked the Church of England, focusing on its role in education and its inculcation of insincerity, and calling for its 'euthanasia' – the Church would experience a 'pleasant death' as the clergy died off and were not replaced. The second work was *An Analysis of the Influence of Natural Religion on the Temporal Happiness of Mankind*, published in 1822 under the pseudonym Philip Beauchamp. This work was edited by George Grote, an atheist, who would later gain fame as the historian of Greece, and become Vice-Chancellor of the University of London. It was based on manuscripts which Bentham headed 'Jug. Util.' The abbreviation 'Jug.' stood for 'Juggernaut', which was Bentham's nickname for religion. Like the huge carriage which carried the idol of Krishna, under whose wheels devotees were said to throw themselves, religion crushed any one who came under its influence.

'Util.' referred simply to utility. Hence 'Jug. Util.' was concerned with the utility of religion – whether or not a belief in religion was conducive to happiness.

It is worth pausing to explain what Bentham understood by religious belief. A believer in religion – a religionist – was an individual who assumed

> the existence of an invisible and superhuman being, by whom provision has been made of a system of rewards and punishments to be eventually administered to individuals of the human species – either in the present, or in a future, life, or in both.

Religion was either natural or revealed. Both revealed and natural religionists believed that the invisible and superhuman being, or someone in communication with that being, had laid down a rule of conduct, together with a system of rewards and punishments. The former, however, believed that the supernatural being had laid down the rule 'in a determinate body of discourse' which was 'at this present time perceptible and, in a degree adequate to that same purpose, intelligible', while the latter did not believe in the existence of any such discourse.[3] A Christian revealed religionist, for instance, would take the Bible, while a natural religionist would take a study of the natural world – God's creation – as the foundation for his belief.

Analysis of the Influence of Natural Religion, then, dealt with the consequences to be expected from a belief in the existence of a God whose nature had to be inferred from the characteristics of a physical world which, it was assumed, the God had created. The key question was whether a belief in an afterlife, where an all-powerful God distributed pains and pleasures, produced 'happiness or misery in the present life'.[4] The short answer was – misery, and a great deal of it. The third work was *Not Paul, but Jesus*, which appeared in 1823 under the pseudonym Gamaliel Smith. This work was edited by Francis Place, the 'radical tailor', and, like Grote, an atheist, though Place appears to have been much more faithful to Bentham's original manuscripts than Grote. Comparing the teachings and activities of Paul with those of Jesus, Bentham argued that the religion of Paul differed significantly from that of Jesus. In particular, while Jesus was in many respects a hedonist, Paul was very much an ascetic. Paul was an impostor and a fraud, intent on gaining control over the nascent Christian movement on account of the power, wealth and reputation he calculated it would bring him.

After Bentham's death, the publication of an edition of his *Works*, as we have seen in Chapter Two,[5] was entrusted to John Bowring. There is some irony in the appointment of Bowring as Bentham's literary executor, in that Bowring, a merchant by profession, a linguist and translator of poetry, was also a Unitarian and a hymn-writer. One of his hymns, still regularly sung today, is *In the cross of Christ I glory*, which puts a utilitarian gloss on the passion:

> Bane and blessing, pain and pleasure,
> By the cross are sanctified;
> Peace is there that knows no measure,
> Joys that through all time abide.

In defiance of the instructions left by Bentham in his will,[6] Bowring did not include any of the 'Jug. Util.' material in the *Works*. He also omitted all three of Bentham's published works on religion, on the grounds that he did not wish to alienate potential readers. Bowring, having completed the *Works*, deposited the bulk of Bentham's manuscripts in University College, London Library, but not the 'Jug. Util.' manuscripts. Bentham bequeathed these manuscripts, consisting in around 1,500 folios, to Harriet Grote, the wife of George. They were eventually acquired by the British Library as part of the Grote Papers. They have remained virtually unknown, a fact not unrelated to the difficulty of reading Bentham's handwriting. The manuscripts were written between 1811 and 1821, when Bentham was in his sixties and seventies; as he got older, his eyes got worse, and his handwriting – his 'scrawl' as he often referred to it – suffered accordingly. He worked on them at his country retreat, the glorious Ford Abbey in Devon, where he spent over half his time between July 1814 and February 1818 (the compensation money from the panopticon scheme paid the rent). That an ancient abbey was the location where he collaborated on such a scandalous project – with his atheistic friends James Mill and Francis Place working alongside him in a room adorned with Mortlake tapestries showing scenes from the life of the Apostle Paul – no doubt appealed to Bentham's sense of humour.

Bentham envisaged that 'Jug. Util.' would be published under the title of 'The usefulness of Religion to the present life examined'.

The work had two objects: the first was to remove a direct source of misery, by freeing individuals from fear of supernatural punishment; the second was to remove the support which oppressive governments received from religion.[7] To this end, Bentham would distinguish between natural and revealed religion, and between the questions of the usefulness and the truth (or 'verity') of religion. In the first place he would show that neither natural nor revealed religion promoted happiness. He would then turn to verity, and having made the general case against the truth of all revelations, he would investigate the truth of the religion of Jesus, and in particular show that Jesus had no 'supernatural commission'.[8] He would go on to show that the religion of Jesus did not promote happiness, but had been adopted and used for political purposes. The work would be completed by a history of Jesus' life and a history of the Jewish nation up to the time of Jesus.[9] The extent to which the manuscripts in the Grote Papers match up to the proposed plan is not yet clear, so rather than trying to organize the discussion below according to this plan, I have concentrated on arguments which seem very relevant either to enduring philosophical questions or to issues which are of interest today.

THE DESIGNER OF THE UNIVERSE

An issue of enormous controversy in the United States of America, and to some extent even in the more overtly secular United Kingdom, is the question of the origin of the universe, with Christian fundamentalists – the creationists – rejecting the theory of the Big Bang and the theory of evolution and appealing instead to the notion of intelligent design. This position is, in essence, a reiteration of the natural theology prevalent in the eighteenth and early nineteenth centuries, and given one of its classic statements in William Paley's *Natural Theology*, published in 1802. According to Paley, if you were to walk across a field and kick your foot against a stone, you would think nothing more of it. However, were you to discover a watch, you would recognize that it had been designed to fulfil a particular purpose. From the existence of a design, you would be led to infer the existence of a designer. By analogy, if you studied the natural world, you would find design everywhere. The natural world had a designer, who was God. The fact that the natural world teemed with joyous life was evidence of the designer's benevolence. God wanted his creatures to be happy, hence it was our moral duty to promote the happiness of God's creatures. In order to enforce this moral duty, God would distribute pains and pleasures in an afterlife, punishing those who had disobeyed his will and behaved badly, and rewarding those who had followed his will and behaved well.[10]

Bentham engaged with Paley at several levels, and on several occasions, during his career. It is tempting to think that Bentham had Paley's argument in favour of intelligent design in mind when he wrote:

> So far is the existence of a punishing and rewarding almighty creator from being demonstrated or demonstrable, that the contrary is not only demonstrable but demonstrated. Punishment and remuneration suppose design: design, makers: makers, sensibility to pain as well as pleasure: pain and pleasure, a nervous system. The supposition of the existence of the sort of being in question involves in it, therefore, a multitude of self-contradictory propositions.[11]

In other words, the idea of a supernatural being who possessed a natural body, an assumption to which the creationists had no option but to commit themselves if they accepted a future dispensation, was an absurdity.

Bentham deployed several further objections against the notion that the universe had a creator. If it was argued that things did not possess the power themselves to come into existence, and, therefore, required a person to create them, it might then be asked, how did this creating person come into existence? This would require a person even more powerful, since he had to create not only the things themselves, but also a person powerful enough to create those things. But then again, queried Bentham, if the creator was powerful enough to exist of himself, why not the things? It was easier to conceive of 'a set of things existing by themselves' than to conceive of the existence of 'those same things' with the addition of 'a person to bring them into existence'. Bentham noted that the religionists assumed that this creator had, before his creation of things, existed in solitude. How long had he existed in this state, and why had he ended it?

> Was it that at last he grew tired of it, and found himself in want of amusement – and for his amusement created that whole of

which so minute a part is open to our view? created this world, as an ingenious child that wanted something to play with might create his play things?'

Bentham confessed that the idea that our world had no beginning seemed 'very strange', but, he continued, the idea of its having a beginning was equally strange. No one had ever been a 'percipient witness' to the beginning of the world, so 'why say that it must have had a beginning?' The typical process of reasoning was as follows: 'Each individual object . . . has had a beginning: therefore, every one has: therefore, all have: therefore, the whole has.' (This is what logicians call the fallacy of composition.) But in order to say that our world had a beginning, we would need to have had experience of a number of worlds each of which had been created at a particular point of time. If all these worlds had a creator, or the same creator, we might properly conclude that there was a degree of probability that our world had been created in the same way.

> But suppose . . . that the world never was created: had existed from all eternity, going on as we see it. What we see is a succession of events and stages of things taking place one after another: such being the case at this time, why not at any other and at every other time?[12]

In other words, if we confined ourselves to experience and observation – the only basis for knowledge – the one state of affairs which made sense to us was that of a process – that of one thing happening after another.

THE PROBLEM OF PERSONAL IDENTITY

The central message of Christianity is that because of Jesus' sacrifice of his life (Bentham wondered why Christians objected so strongly to suicide, given the example of Jesus), human beings have been granted the opportunity to gain the favour of the Almighty, and thereby access to a state of eternal bliss. This, for Bentham, raised an insuperable problem: how could the human beings which existed in this world be identical with the human beings which existed in the supposed future world? Religionists had adopted two lines of argument: the first was that, after the death of the individual, the

Almighty created a new body for the soul to inhabit (the resurrection of the dead); the second was that the soul continued to exist without the body (the immortality of the soul).[13] In this latter case, Bentham noted that during life human beings experienced sensation and thought, and that such sensation and thought was located in the brain and nervous system. At death, however, both brain and nervous system ceased to function. Bentham asked: 'A mind altogether without body, in what sense, respect or degree is it to be identical with the same mind united with its body as in the present state?' Mind (a fictitious entity) consisted in nothing more than a combination of pleasures, pains, wants, desires and propensities. All the pleasures and pains of the mind had their source in pleasures and pains of the body. How were these wants to be supplied, desires gratified, and propensities given way to, by a mind without a body? This 'pure mind', without a body,

> what pleasures can it indulge, what gratifications can it propose to itself, what pursuits embark on – pursuits for which no object can be found? Existences – modes of being – in every respect so compleatly different, in what respect can one of them be considered as being the continuation of the other?

These were not merely difficulties to be overcome, argued Bentham, but 'objections absolutely insuperable'.

If the soul or mind of a man was supposed to be identical to the whole man of which, during life, it had formed a part, there arose the problem as to just which 'of the states through which the man had passed' it was to be identical – at what age, in what state of health, and in what mental capacity? Suppose that the man, before his death, and through no moral failing on his part, had, in body and mind, 'existed in a state of comparative insensibility, little elevated above absolute insensibility or non-existence', was this to be 'the whole man of which the mental part is to be the copy or continuance?' A man who had been mentally retarded from birth, would he continue to be mentally retarded in a future life? If not, where was the identity?

The same questions could be asked about bodily resurrection. Take a man who had lived through to 'decrepit old age', sometimes in health, sometimes in illness. At which age, and in what condition of health or illness, would he appear in his second self? If he had lost his sight in his first self, would he be blind in his second self, and blind for eternity? Would an infant who died at the breast remain at the breast for all eternity? Or would his second self be at some other age, for instance 25 years' old. But in that case, 'where is the identity between the man of 25 and the infant of 6 months? His second self, what can it recollect of its former self? if nothing, then what is become of the identity?'[14]

In an argument reminiscent of that deployed by Peter Singer against 'speciesism' in his controversial book *Practical Ethics*,[15] Bentham noted that although the attribute of a soul and thence of immortality had seldom been extended to animals beyond the human species, a well-trained dog – not to speak of a monkey, a horse or an elephant – was superior in its intellectual faculties to a human child some days or even weeks after his birth. 'Is a separate being – an immortal soul – necessary to keep in exercise the inferior faculties of the biped, and shall it be less necessary to keep in exercise the superior faculties of the quadruped?' But if dogs and horses were in possession of an immortal soul, at what point 'in the scale of brutal talent shall the faculty of existing stop?'

> If degree of intelligence is to be the criterion, the characteristic mark by which the point of separation between mortality and immortality is indicated, what is clear beyond all possibility of denial is that instances in abundance are not wanting in which, by the criterion, immortality would be shewn to be the lot of the brute – of the non-human animal, mortality of the human.

A further question was – what would these souls be doing – 'what sublime and refined occupations' would these 'naked souls' be involved in? All the ideas of even 'the most profound and abstraction-loving philosopher' were derived from perceptions of the physical world, and these perceptions were received through the body. His soul would need another such body in order to possess any ideas at all. If it was said that the ideas which the soul acquired when joined with its body would remain with it, 'what can it do with them? in what way will it be the better for them? what occupation can they, all of them put together, find for it?'

> A Palladio, what will he be the better for all the ideas of his palaces that he succeeded in forming to himself and in lodging in

his mind? what stones will he have to build with? or Raphael for his ideas of pictures? or Handel for his ideas of Symphonies and Songs? or Marlborough for his ideas of battles and sieges?

The same could be said of the humble tailor, shoemaker, weaver or orange seller.[16] In short, we were material creatures; whatever exists in a supposed non-material world could not be us.

ETERNAL LIFE VERSUS NON-EXISTENCE

If there were no such thing as a future life, noted Bentham, we would be left with the prospect of 'non-existence'. Such a prospect was not 'by any means an uncomfortable one'. Non-existence was merely '[t]he state we were in before we were born' and in which we re-entered 'as often as, without dreaming, we have been sleeping'. Non-existence was a more comfortable thought than that of eternal suffering. Religion presented the ultimate gamble – the option between everlasting enjoyment and 'boundless torment'. No one in his senses, argued Bentham, if he had a choice, would play such a game. If the state of death was an evil, it must be because it was a state in which there was experience of pain or loss of pleasure. It was obvious, however, that the fear of suffering pain, and by the same token the loss of pleasure, after death was 'a mere illusion'. The illusion was based on the thought that all the things which we enjoyed in the present life would be lost to us forever. This was to confuse the idea of non-existence with the idea of 'a sort of dull and melancholy existence', that is, a state in which such losses would be felt. When a friend died, a man felt loss; he assumed that after his own death, he would lose all his friends at one and the same time. The fact was that he would not experience any sadness. In order to feel sadness, a man had to exist – but the man had no existence.

> Sadness? what sadness did you feel last night when, being asleep, no one of all these friends were with you, nor had you present in your mind any expectation of ever seeing any of them more? As little will you when you are dead: death is neither more nor less than sleep in which there is no dream, and which will never end.

If death was not, potentially, such a terrible thing, there was no reason to forbid a person from choosing it. Some of 'the modes of quitting the present existence' were 'sadly afflictive', but 'easy ones in abundance are at a man's desire: deaths so easy that before there can be any time for feeling, feeling is no more'.[17] In Bentham's view, it was prejudice engendered by religion which had led legislators to prohibit an individual from taking his own life, which was the perfectly reasonable course when life had become intolerable. It need hardly be said how Bentham's argument resonates today in relation to the debate on euthanasia.

Moreover, the much-trumpeted future state of eternal bliss might not turn out to be so attractive after all. Bentham noted that the two most important groups of pleasures in this world were those of the bed and of the table – in other words, sex, and food and drink. Yet these were the pleasures which the religionists excluded from a future life because they considered them 'gross'. It seemed that all they expected people to do in heaven was to stroll around looking at flowers, listening to music and chatting to each other.[18]

THE REVEALED RELIGION OF JESUS

Adherents of the religion of Jesus made the claim, noted Bentham, that it was not only true, but also a moral system of 'matchless utility'. Bentham disagreed. Jesus did not produce any systematic thought; he was not motivated by benevolence; and his doctrines, if applied literally, would subvert government and destroy society. Bentham focused on the Sermon on the Mount, considered to be the essential collection of Jesus' moral teachings. The so-called Golden Rule, Jesus' celebrated precept 'do as you would be done by',[19] would, if acted upon consistently, argued Bentham, be 'subversive of all Government'. What it amounted to saying was, 'do good to every man and do evil to no man', and as such would condemn all coercion, all punishment, and, therefore, all government.[20] Any act of government necessarily produced evil, since it necessarily involved coercion. But such action was right in so far as it produced more good than evil. Whether government operated by punishment or reward – and there were no other means by which it could operate – it did evil. Punishment was evil, and to punish intentionally was to inflict evil intentionally. Evil was produced where compensation, exacted from the wrongdoer, was paid to the person wronged. Evil was produced whenever a contract was entered into, insofar as an obligation regarded as burdensome was imposed on one of the parties. Evil was produced whenever a road, canal, port, fortification or government building was constructed. Evil was produced whenever taxation was imposed. Evil was produced whenever government bestowed a reward, for instance, when it paid a salary to an official. The money which constituted the salary had to be collected from individuals within the community, and to those individuals, the payment of the tax was an evil.[21] The Golden Rule was, however, 'much less dangerous', and 'much more purely, if not extensively, useful' when understood as 'a rule of prudence' (though Bentham did not think that Jesus viewed it in this way). The point was to consider how, in your dealings with others, you would like to be treated, if you were in their situation. This would be likely to produce goodwill on their part towards you.[22]

Bentham was convinced that the doctrines propounded by Jesus in the Sermon on the Mount, if applied generally, would be destructive of society. Jesus' sayings along the lines of taking no thought for the morrow[23] were '*dicta* inculcative of improvidence and idleness'. A further set of precepts advocated disinterestedness and meekness.[24] Jesus' purpose was not 'universal and permanent peace', but rather 'to sow discord, and the most mischievous and remediless of discords', as he expressly admitted.[25] Indeed, the combination of 'passive resignation and active beneficence' – if someone wants your shirt, give him your coat as well – would result in the ultimate discord, namely the destruction of property.[26] Under the levelling system, where the whole property of a community would be equally divided among its members, each person would still retain an equal pittance. But under Jesus' system, the whole property of the community 'would be in the hands of malefactors and persons into whose hands it had passed from the hands of malefactors'.[27]

Bentham pointed out that it was common for these doctrines to be defended on the very grounds of their 'extravagance'. Taken literally, the doctrines were 'too extravagant to have ever been entertained by any human being not in a state of mental derangement', and, therefore, they were not meant to be taken literally. I am reminded of a scene from the film *Monty Python's Life of Brian*. The characters, towards the back of the crowd, are straining to listen to Jesus who is delivering the Sermon on the Mount. Distracted by two men arguing about whether one of them has a big nose, a wealthy Jew misses Jesus' remark, and asks: 'What's that?' A man, a little further up the hill, turns round and says: 'I think it was – blessed are the cheese makers.' The rich Jew's wife disdainfully remarks, 'What's so special about the cheese makers?', to which her husband replies: 'It's not meant to be taken literally. It refers to any manufacturers of any dairy products.' If the precepts were not to be taken literally, but to be interpreted, what this amounted to, noted Bentham, was the claim that the words in which they were expressed had to be replaced by some other words in order to make them comprehendible. This gave rise to the following absurdity:

> Here is a God, an omniscient being, who, having laws to declare – laws having for their end in view the giving direction to human conduct, knows not how to express himself – instead of the terms proper to the design and capable of giving effect to it, employs terms that are improper, terms not capable of producing that effect: whereupon the design remains, as it could not but do, without any effect for many ages. Here on the other hand is a man [i.e. the interpreter] who, though but a man, knows what the omniscient God does not know, knows what the words are which are capable of producing that effect which the God, though thus long labouring to produce, has thus long been unable to produce.[28]

Bentham's point is that an unintelligible revelation is a contradiction in terms. Further proof that the interpreters chose whatever meaning suited them, noted Bentham, came from the fact that when Jesus did speak figuratively at the Last Supper, likening the bread to his body and the wine to his blood, the established churches took it in a literal sense. Hence, at the service of holy communion, the bread and wine were transformed into the actual body and blood of Christ.[29]

JESUS' REAL PURPOSE

Jesus was not, in Bentham's view, a madman. The confusion originated with those of his followers and 'votaries' who had found an advantage in setting themselves up as the interpreters of God's word, and who had been blinded to the actual purpose of the historical Jesus – to the true history of his career and that of the movement which had emerged after his death. Bentham pointed out that the phrase in the Lord's Prayer 'thy kingdom come' alluded to

> the grand and long-sighed-for consummation which every Jewish eye was at that time, and for a long time before had been, upon the look out for, viz. the coming of King Messiah: the coming of the continually promised hero under whose command the whole people were to change their condition from that of oppressed vassals to that of conquerors and rulers.

Jesus' followers tried to propagate the view that Jesus would be the one to wear the 'crown of gold', but when things went awry, the 'crown of thorns' took its place, 'and the kingdom which with one voice the prophets had proclaimed a temporal, was found to be but a spiritual, one'.[30]

Jesus was admired for promoting the 'affections of the social class' – humility, self-denial, benevolence and beneficence – but, argued Bentham, Jesus had no other object than advancing his 'own project of temporal ambition'. In order to place himself on the throne, he needed followers, both rich and poor, the former to supply money, and the latter to constitute a military force. Hence, Jesus preached a system of improvidence – what every man had was to be given away, and no thought was to be taken for the morrow. Wealth would be taken from the owner, and given to the poor – which meant to his own followers, and thereby to Jesus himself, since, with the exception of 'preaching – preaching subjection to himself . . . trade he had none, and poor in a very sufficient degree it would every now and then happen to him to be'. While the system Jesus preached would have been 'certainly and immediately destructive' of human society in general, it suited his own particular purpose. His followers would inevitably have squabbled among themselves. He had no police force that he could use to suppress these disputes. Had he taken sides with one party as opposed to another, he would have disastrously weakened his movement, and made his objective still more difficult to achieve. His 'sole resource' was to plant 'the most perfect system of self-abjection – a disposition to claim nothing – to yield every thing – to give every thing that any one could be found to accept – to aim at no advantage – to resent no injury – and to make sure of the not resenting it, even to court it'. Given the existence of disputes and disagreements among his closest followers, no doubt ambitious for pre-eminence and distinction when Jesus eventually established his authority, the only course which he could take was to preach humility – to tell them that the only way they could gain his favour was not through competing to be first, but to be last – not to be the greatest, but the least. The renunciation of ambition and vengeance, and the exchange of indigence for affluence, were policies perfectly adapted to the peculiar situation in which Jesus found himself, but not, of course, to the situation of society in general. As Bentham wryly observed, the early nineteenth-century interpreters of Jesus hardly took his doctrines on poverty seriously – the clergy were not short on ambition when a Bishopric or an Archbishopric became vacant.[31]

If Jesus had wished to promote the happiness of mankind during the present life, and had been guided by 'that degree of intelligence and wisdom of which human reason without any assistance from religion – without any assistance supernaturally given by and received from God – is susceptible', he would have gone about his task in a very different way. He would have described those actions which produced preponderant evil; those which were legally prohibited and punished he would have termed crimes or misdemeanours; and those not so dealt with, he would have termed moral offences or, if liable to punishment by God by supernatural means, whether in the present or a future life, sins. He would have considered in which cases it would not have been advisable to attach punishment, and in those cases where it was applicable, he would have considered the quantity and quality of the punishment proper to be applied. He would have shown the way in which moral offences tended to produce ill-will towards their perpetrators, and the relative mischievousness of various transgressions, thereby advising persons in general what degree of ill-will they ought to show towards such transgressions. In case of sins, he might have attempted to indicate the amount of supernatural punishment which God would allocate to the various sins which he had identified.[32] In other words, he should have written *An Introduction to the Principles of Morals and Legislation*, albeit with an extra chapter or two on sins and the religious sanction.

ASCETICISM AND JESUS' SEXUALITY

According to Bentham, the teaching of the Christian Church supported the principle of asceticism, which was the opposite of the principle of utility. Whereas the proponent of the principle of utility approved of those actions which produced pleasure and averted pain, the proponent of the principle of asceticism approved of those actions which produced pain and averted pleasure. The principle of asceticism had typically been embraced by a 'religious party', whose motivation for so doing was 'the fear of future punishment at the hands of a splenetic and revengeful Deity'.[33] Bentham aimed to show that, despite its claims to the contrary, the Christian Church had, in the teachings of Jesus, no warrant for its disapproval of pleasure, and for the practices by which its adherents inflicted pain on themselves. Jesus himself did not, on any occasion, condemn 'the pleasures of the table' – the consumption of palatable food and drink – or 'the pleasures of the bed' – the indulgence of the sexual appetite. In Bentham's view, Paul had been responsible for introducing asceticism into the Christian religion. The Christian religion had, in fact, very little in common with the historical Jesus in terms of its attitude towards sex.

Bentham noted that at no point did Jesus condemn, either in words or in action, the sexual activities of Mary Magdalene, whose 'profession' was that of prostitute. (Bentham assumes that the Mary who anoints Jesus in John 12.2–8 is Mary Magdalene, as is the 'woman . . . which was a sinner' who anoints Jesus in Luke 7.36–50, a view long accepted by the Church, but not by modern biblical scholars.) Mary Magdalene was 'represented as living with [Jesus], from the day of her reception into the number of his votaries to the day of his death and even afterwards, upon terms of the closest attachment and strictest intimacy'. The Gospel writers – 'the four biographers of Jesus' as Bentham referred to them – did not suggest that there had been any 'sexual union' between the two of them, but, Bentham speculated, there would have been no reason for them to have mentioned it, unless they had produced children.[34] Though Bentham did not say this explicitly, he intimates that Mary Magdalene was the Gospel equivalent of the gangster's moll, or the rock star's groupie, and possibly the groupie for the whole band.[35]

Nor did Jesus, claimed Bentham, at any point condemn homosexuality. Bentham recognized that the ascetic might respond that Jesus had no need to condemn such 'abominations' explicitly, because they stood condemned in the Mosaic law, that the two cities of Sodom and Gomorrah had been destroyed on this account, and that 'the law by which such vengeance was, by almighty ben-evolence, attached to such inconceivably disgusting and unpardon-ably eccentric taste' was, therefore, 'universal' and 'eternal'. This was precisely the claim Blackstone had made in *Commentaries on the Laws of England*:

> This [the crime of nature] the voice of nature and of reason, and the express law of God,[36] determine to be capital. Of which we have a signal instance, long before the Jewish dispensation, by the destruction of two cities by fire from heaven: so that this is an universal, not merely a provincial, precept.[37]

Bentham's response was to point out that the two cities had not been destroyed merely because of an *'error loci'* in respect of sex, but rather through the non-consensual nature of the sexual acts in question – it was akin to the difference between 'simple fornication' and rape. Bentham noted that homosexual acts were punishable by death under the Mosaic law, as was bestiality – 'a mistake of sex' as well as 'a mistake of species' – and even where the sex and the species were correct, but there was 'a simple mistake of times and seasons', the punishment was severe.[38] But in the Mosaic law, imagination had run riot and punishment had been attached to a wide variety of actions regarded by his contemporaries as innocu-ous, such as weaving or wearing linsey-woolsey, sowing different grains in the same field, and ploughing with an ox and ass together,[39] while capital offences included fornication on the part of a priest's daughter,[40] adultery if caught in the act,[41] cursing one's father or mother,[42] and sabbath breaking.[43] In short, either one adhered to the whole of the Mosaic law, or admitted that it did not constitute an appropriate standard of right and wrong.

Bentham's argument here anticipates that put forward by the Roman Catholic priest John J. McNeill in *The Church and the Homosexual*, published in 1976. McNeill points out that the story of Sodom and Gomorrah was the most important biblical basis for the Christian tradition of the condemnation of homosexuality. The author of the account did not, however, suggest that the cities were destroyed on account of the homosexuality of their inhabit-ants, but rather for their sinfulness in general, and in particular for their pride and inhospitality.[44] McNeill, furthermore, suggests that Paul did not condemn homosexuality as such (Bentham would

have disagreed with him here),[45] and goes on to discuss Christ's attitude to sexuality:

> The point I am trying to make here is, obviously, not that Christ
> was a homosexual – any more than he was a heterosexual . . . –
> but rather, that he was an extraordinarily full human person and
> an extraordinarily free human being.[46]

Bentham, as we have seen in relation to Mary Magdalene and shall
now see in relation to members of the male sex, was not so quick to
dismiss the physicality of Jesus's sexuality, and would have enjoyed
a wry smile at the thought that sexual activity might not constitute
an important ingredient in what it meant to be 'an extraordinarily
full human person' and 'an extraordinarily free human being'.

As noted above, Bentham pointed out that Jesus did not condemn
homosexuality. He went on to suggest that there was evidence that
Jesus was himself a practising homosexual. Bentham was intrigued
by an incident which is related in Mark, but not in any of the other
Gospels. The incident described in this passage took place in the
Garden of Gethsemane, after Jesus had been betrayed by Judas (by
a kiss – not that this in itself proved anything, admitted Bentham,
since such behaviour, while not acceptable in England, would not
have been regarded as indecent in antiquity, as it would not have
been in Europe) and seized by the armed 'police of Jerusalem'
sent by the chief priests, scribes and elders. According to Mark's
account, one of Jesus' followers cut off the ear of one of the servants
of the high priest, whereupon Jesus made a comment to the effect
that he was prepared to surrender peacefully. Mark continues:
'they [referring to Jesus' followers] all forsook him and fled'. Then
comes the incident which intrigued Bentham, rendered thus in the
Authorized Version:

> And there followed him a certain young man, having a linen
> cloth cast about his naked body; and the young men laid hold on
> him: And he left the linen cloth, and fled from them naked.[47]

Bentham noted that 'some Commentators' had suggested that the
young man was a male prostitute,[48] an interpretation with which
Bentham found it difficult to disagree – why otherwise characterize him by 'the looseness of his attire'? The fact that he was said

to be clothed in linen showed that the young man was not poor, since linen, manufactured in Egypt, was 'rare and dear'. There was much that was obscure in the passage, short though it was, noted Bentham. Who were the young men who laid hold of him? What was their purpose in so doing – was it 'hostile or amorous'? Whatever the case, Bentham was further perplexed by the translation in the Authorized Version of one particular word, which, he claimed, put a different gloss on the affair than the original Greek. According to the Authorized Version, the young man 'followed' Jesus. This implied that it was only after the rest of his followers had fled, and Jesus was in the hands of the Jerusalem 'police', that the young man for the first time joined Jesus. However, the original Greek stated that the young man 'was following' Jesus. (Bentham's point is confirmed by modern translations.) What the original Greek implied was that the young man continued to follow Jesus, despite the desertion of all the other followers, including the disciples Peter, James and John. Bentham noted that not only did Jesus not condemn the young man's profession, but allowed him to continue among his followers, in full knowledge that this was his profession (if the fact was noticed by the biographer Mark, it could not have escaped Jesus' attention). This was an occasion, noted Bentham, which gave Jesus an ideal opportunity to condemn homosexuality, had he wished to do so. On the other hand, had 'his own mode of life . . . been such as to render him habitually or occasionally a partaker of it', there was no reason why he should have actively recommended it – 'pleasure in whatever form it presents itself has no need of being preached'.[49] The Gospels, then, suggested that prostitutes, female and male, belonged to Jesus' inner circle, and there was the distinct possibility, in Bentham's view, that Jesus enjoyed the pleasures of the bed with both.

Bentham argued that further evidence of Jesus' active homosexuality came from the account given in John's Gospel of the Last Supper, where one of the disciples, whose name is not mentioned, is described as follows: 'Now there was leaning on Jesus' bosom one of his disciples, whom Jesus loved.'[50] Two verses later, this disciple is found 'lying on Jesus' breast'.[51] It was unlikely that Jesus' biographers would have recorded anything more explicit than this, even if they had knowledge of 'any familiarity more decisive'. But even if they had been explicit, Jesus' 'votaries of the present age' would not have allowed any literal sense to be given to the account, but would have 'spiritualized' it. Just like the 'companion to the heroine of Solomon's Song', the young man with the loose attire would have been regarded as a metaphor for the Church.[52] In the same way, the Last Supper had been given a 'spiritual' meaning, whereas the plain sense was that Jesus, having become aware that the authorities were preparing to crush 'his revolutionary enterprize' and to execute him, was merely asking his followers to remember him. It was natural, argued Bentham, that the leader of a rebellion characterized by 'open disobedience and resistance to the law' should tell his followers that it was for them that his blood would be shed. Jesus had shared bread and wine among his followers, likening them to his body and blood respectively:

> Yet on this social effusion of friendship, thus natural, thus of itself, when understood upon any rational principle, so perfectly clear of every[thing] marvellous, under the impression of awe and terror, in some minds seconded perhaps by fraud, the appetite for the marvellous has laid hold, and out of it made a pretended source of damnation, and a real instrument of pernicious, tyrannic government.

Bentham pointed out that Alexander the Great had publicly caressed the Persian eunuch Bagoas, and that Alexander the Impostor had established a seraglio with youths of both sexes, without being condemned in their own time, and without their lovers being 'spiritualized'.[53]

Bentham did not, of course, need to prove anything about Jesus' sexual inclinations or activities. His point was that there was no basis in the accounts of Jesus' life and teaching for the asceticism which characterized the teaching of the Christian Church. As with most other subjects, Bentham wanted us to rethink and reformulate our attitudes towards sex. He wanted us to realize that the distinction between the 'regular' gratification of the sexual appetite – between one male and one female, and leading to procreation – and the 'irregular' gratification – between male and male, between female and female, between human and beast, between dead and living (I will not go on) – had no basis in 'nature', but was a social construct. Insofar as the respective parties were consenting, and no one came to any harm, then each person should be allowed to practice whatever mode of sexual gratification they chose. He did favour marriage, but he did not have a Christian view of marriage. To the question, what was the difference between a prostitute and a wife? his answer was – 'the length of the contract'. Marriage should not be the lifelong commitment which the Church had made it, but entered into for such specific time as suited the contracting parties.

BENTHAM'S MESSAGE

Bentham's position, which he had outlined as early as the 1770s, was that natural religion was incapable of providing a certain rule of conduct and a known scheme of reward and punishment. In order for society to exist, and for human beings to flourish, it was necessary to have known rules of conduct, and known sanctions in case of non-compliance. The idea of a supernatural being, as posited by the proponents of natural religion, could provide neither known rules nor known sanctions – in other words, theology was not an adequate basis for security. The best that one could do, assuming that God was benevolent, was to hope that he would not punish any act which promoted happiness. But in that case, the standard of rectitude was utility – 'the happiness of this life'. In short, morality and law should be divorced from religion.[54] The religionists, however, insisted that reflection on the nature of the divine should be the foundation of all thought and practice. But what, after all, was the nature of the Christian God?

> The God of the Christians was an inconceivable triple monster in comparison of which the Chimæra of the Greeks – a lion, a serpent and a goat – was beauty, and the three-bodied Gorgon simplicity: a father, with or without a body – a son with a body – and a Ghost without a body, but of the shape of a pigeon, all in one. In the domains of Catholicism, the solitude of the divine monster received a faint alleviation from the accession of an anomalous human being of the female sex. But, as without prejudice to her virginity, she had been on earth a mother, so was she, and so she is doomed for ever to continue in heaven, a sort of sub-Goddess: of no use to the rest of the company in any other character than that of a servant.[55]

An old man, a failed revolutionary, accompanied by a maid servant who had been impregnated by the former, yet remained a virgin, and had given birth to the latter, plus a pigeon – the wonder was not that it made no sense, but that people allowed themselves to be terrified – and terrorized – by it.

Bentham wanted his contemporaries to rethink their whole attitude towards morals and legislation, but knew that they could not do this in a way which would promote well-being until they had put aside or isolated the teachings of religion, whether natural or revealed. This message retains much of its impact today – not only in relation to attitudes towards 'irregularities' of the sexual appetite, though at least in England homosexual males are no longer subject to the death penalty as they were in Bentham's time, but to those aspects of religious thought which remain so influential in many other areas of life. Bentham tells us that all our discourse concerning the religious and supernatural is nonsense – since all knowledge is rooted in our sense-perception of the natural world, there can be no knowledge of the supernatural, and hence all that is said of the supernatural is nonsense. Yet many practices and ideas which are still of fundamental importance to our social life are rooted in religion – much of our moral code and its legal enforcement, including the institution of marriage, our attitudes to such issues as suicide and euthanasia, and the very existence of organized churches, whether state supported or not, not to mention the notions of human dignity and human rights. Bentham's message, buried deep in these obscure manuscripts, is that the juggernaut which is religion needs to be excised from our thinking about morality and law, and replaced – not by some form of moral intuitionism, and not by metaphysics of any sort – but by reflection on how our proposed actions contribute towards the well-being of the sentient creatures whom they will affect. Bentham presents us with a profound challenge – not to the fact that we value life, but to the way in which we value it.

CHAPTER SEVEN

TORTURE

THE TORTURE CASE

On 8 December 2005 the British judges known as the Lords of Appeal delivered their opinions in the 'landmark' torture case denominated A (FC) *v.* Secretary of State for the Home Office, which revolved around the admissibility, in a British court, of evidence obtained in a foreign country, without complicity on the part of the British authorities, by means of torture.[1] The British government wished to use such evidence in the trial of a terrorist suspect, but the judges unanimously agreed that it was inadmissible. They drew on two main sources of justification: the Common Law of England and various declarations of rights, in particular the European Convention on Human Rights. This would have perplexed Bentham, since he was both a stern critic of the Common Law and of metaphysical notions of rights. In this chapter I will assess the extent to which Bentham's criticisms of the British legal and political system remain relevant today. I will also show that he does not condemn the practice of torture in the absolute terms which today's supporters of human rights demand that we should, but allows it some scope in certain circumstances. As we have seen in Chapter Three,[2] Bentham's utilitarianism rules out nothing *a priori*, but requires us to consider every issue on its merits. The appeal to absolute standards is often presented as a sign of virtue, but, from Bentham's perspective, such an appeal merely reinforces prejudice, and is a device for avoiding serious thought.

The main sources on which the Lords of Appeal draw in order to justify their opinions, as noted above, are the Common Law and various declarations of human rights. Bentham would have argued that neither the Common Law nor purported declarations of human rights could provide a justification for anything. Both faced the same ontological problem – neither existed in any meaningful sense. First, take the Common Law. The lawyer, according to Bentham, had created 'a sort of God or Goddess upon Earth, a sort of Divinity which he calls Common Law', but the problem was that the Common Law did not exist – it was a figment of the lawyer's imagination.[3] The fact was that in order to have an aggregate, one needed to have a number of individuals to form that aggregate. There was no such thing as *a* common law. If there was no single common law, there was no aggregate thing that corresponded to the words Common Law.[4]

The Lords of Appeal make a great deal of the fact that the Common Law has historically condemned torture and that torture has not been 'legally sanctioned' in England since 1640, when the conciliar courts (i.e. those which emerged from the King's Council), such as Star Chamber, were abolished. Their Lordships' disapproval of conciliar courts does not seem to extend to the Court of Chancery, whose jurisdiction and 'equitable' principles they have inherited. But leaving that aside, according to Lord Bingham, the leading judge in this case, whose opinion stands first and is the most detailed:

> It is . . . clear that from its very earliest days the common law of England sets its face against the use of torture. Its rejection of this practice was indeed hailed as a distinguishing feature of the common law, the subject of proud claims by English jurists.[5]

And the 'proud claims' are echoed by the judges in this case. Bentham might have asked us to look at the state of the English law in the late eighteenth and early nineteenth centuries, when its apologists were pointing out its superiority over other systems in not authorizing the use of torture. This was the time of the Bloody Code. It might have been illegal to subject you to torture (the practice of torturing jurors who had failed to reach a unanimous verdict had fallen into disuse), but in 1820 there were over 200 offences for which you might be hung. In England and Wales in the 5 years from 1821 to 1825 there were 5,220 capital convictions, and 364 executions.[6] Such was the humanity of the Common Law of which our judges today are so 'proud'. Legal procedure was so expensive that only the rich were able to enforce their legal rights. The boast that every one was equal before the law, complained Bentham, was a cruel falsehood.[7]

Bentham would have been interested to hear Lord Carswell announce that the fiction of judges declaring law had been jettisoned.[8] This alludes to the traditional doctrine that judges did not make law, but declared the law – in other words, the law already existed, and it was the role of judges, drawing on their many years' experience, to find the law and declare it to the rest of the community.[9] Bentham would not have thought that Carswell's admission that judges did in fact make law was something to boast of, but was rather a barefaced admission of culpability. What judges made, in Bentham's view, was sham law, *ex-post-facto*-law, dog law. As he explained, the judges made the Common Law in the same way that 'a man makes laws for his dog. When your dog does anything you want to break him of, you wait till he does it, and then beat him for it'. The judges refused to say in advance what a man should not do, but 'lie by till he has done something which they say he should not *have done*, and then they hang him for it'.[10] The Common Law, according to Bentham, was corrupt, unknowable, incomplete and arbitrary. Rather like religion, it could not perform the minimum purpose for which law was instituted – the guidance of conduct. Still less was it able to afford protection to those basic interests of the individual – person, property, reputation and condition in life – which constituted security, and hence a major component of well-being. Carswell goes on to quote with approval the view of Peter de Ponceau that the Common Law 'is by its very nature uncertain and fluctuating'.[11] This echoes the so-called lawyer's toast 'to the glorious uncertainty of the law' which so appalled Bentham. Without certainty, of course, there could be no security, which, as we have seen in Chapter One,[12] was the very point of the law.

The second main source of justification on which the Lords of Appeal rely is the doctrine of human rights. I will treat human rights as the modern equivalent of what, in Bentham's time, were known as natural rights, though it is true that some modern conceptions of human rights attempt to avoid some of the difficulties which Bentham identified with natural rights. Nevertheless, in many respects, to speak of natural rights rather than human rights is only a change of terminology, and not one of any great substance. Bentham had two main objections to the notion of natural rights. The first objection was ontological. Natural rights, like the Common Law, did not exist, insofar as they were conceived to exist independently of government, and therefore of law. A right was the 'child of law',[13] and law had to be made by a legislator. To claim that one possessed something which did not exist was nonsense, but then to claim, as did the French Declaration of the Rights of Man of 1789, that this non-existent thing was 'imprescriptible', or irrevocable, was to mount one nonsense upon another – talk of natural rights was simple nonsense, talk of natural and imprescriptible rights was 'nonsense upon stilts'.[14] The best that could be said for natural rights was that they were moral claims ambiguously stated. It would be far better to use words which expressed exactly what one was aiming to achieve, and therefore to talk about 'securities against misrule'.[15] The second objection was that the legislature had to be left at liberty to act in any way which might be appropriate in the circumstances – the legislature had to be 'omnicompetent'. To try to restrict the field of activity of the legislature by means of such restrictions as were contained in declarations of rights was to claim infallibility. It was to impose the will of the dead on the living – it was to subject the more experienced and thence more knowledgeable generations to those which were less experienced and less knowledgeable. It was fallacy.[16]

THE DOCTRINE OF THE SEPARATION OF POWERS

A great deal of what is said in the opinions of the Lords of Appeal in relation to the admissibility of evidence which has been extracted by torture is made to hang on the doctrine of the separation of powers, and in particular on the distinction between the judicial and executive powers. Information extracted by torture might, they say, be legally used by the executive, but not by the judiciary, as such use would undermine the integrity of the judicial process. This argument only makes sense if the separation of powers doctrine makes sense. Bentham rejected the doctrine of the separation of powers as an inappropriate basis for the organization of government: it was not a security for good government, or, what he regarded as the same thing, a guarantee of constitutional liberty, except in certain accidental circumstances.[17] He did not believe that any benefit was derived from the mere division of the functions of government between several sets of mutually independent officials. For Bentham, the key to good government lay in making rulers dependent on subjects. It was this principle which he developed in his later writings on constitutional law and representative democracy. Good government resulted from the subordination of the legislative power to the people, and of what Bentham termed the administrative power (i.e. what is commonly termed the executive) and of the judicial power to the legislative. This brings me to a related point. For Bentham, both administrative power and judicial power were species of executive power. Ministers and judges exercised the same sort of power, the only difference being that the judicial power was brought into action in response to a requisition from a third party.[18] I appreciate that the argument here needs a great deal of filling out, but the essential point is that if information is good enough to ground action by the administrative (or executive) power, it is good enough to ground action by the judiciary. Or to put this another way, to justify any substantive conclusion on the basis of some supposed distinction between executive and judicial power would be, in Bentham's phrase, to 'deal in sounds instead of sense'.[19]

BENTHAM ON THE EXCLUSION OF EVIDENCE

To the non-lawyer it seems obvious that the torture case is about the admissibility of evidence. That would, however, be too simple for the lawyers who make their fortunes and careers out of these 'landmark' cases. The leading judge in the case, Lord Bingham, tells us what it is really about: 'It trivialises the issue . . . to treat it as an argument about the law of evidence. The issue is one of constitutional principle'.[20] Nevertheless, the seven judges do spend a great deal of time discussing the law of evidence, and in doing so advance the argument that evidence obtained by torture is inherently untrustworthy, and as such should be excluded. I do not have space to discuss in detail Bentham's views on the exclusion of evidence, but suffice it to say that, as William Twining has observed, Bentham's 'general principle' is that 'no evidence should be excluded unless it is irrelevant or superfluous or its production would involve preponderant vexation, expense or delay'.[21] Bentham's arguments went to undermine the view that evidence of certain sorts should be excluded on the grounds of its being 'untrustworthy'. Rather it was the function of the judge to evaluate just what probative force each particular piece of evidence possessed. Twining summarizes Bentham's position as follows:

> Most testimony is true; rigid exclusionary rules tend to exclude much information that is reliable; even false or unreliable evidence is better than no evidence: the former may be useful – for example, in identifying inconsistencies or as indicative evidence leading to other, better evidence. Exclusion is almost always a false security against misdecision. There are other, better, safeguards for securing the completeness and accuracy of testimony (and of other evidence). Thus the exclusion of relevant evidence is unnecessary as a safeguard against deception and is likely to lead to the loss of useful information.[22]

Bentham would not, therefore, exclude evidence obtained by torture on the grounds that it is inherently untrustworthy. An intelligent judge would be able to take a view as to what weight to give to the evidence in question.

THE FOX-HUNTER'S FALLACY

Lord Bingham quotes with approval an opinion delivered in 1846 by the Vice-Chancellor Sir James Lewis Knight-Bruce:

> The discovery and vindication and establishment of truth are main purposes certainly of the existence of Courts of Justice; still for the obtaining of these objects, which however valuable and important, cannot be usefully or creditably pursued unfairly or gained by unfair means, not every channel is or ought to be open to them.[23]

This is reminiscent of Bentham's fox-hunter's fallacy, which he describes not in his writings on political fallacies, but in his writings on judicial evidence. It was one of a number of arguments used by lawyers to support the exclusion of what Bentham called 'self-disserving testimony', and in particular to support the rule that 'no one is bound to accuse himself' (a rule quoted with approval by their Lordships in this case). The fallacy consisted in transferring the sense of fair play from the sporting to the judicial arena. The fox had to have a fair chance for his life – he had to be given a certain distance before he was chased, and he could not be shot once the chase had begun. In sport, where the purpose was amusement, these rules were rational. They introduced an element of delay, otherwise the amusement would be over all too quickly. Moreover, if the fox were hunted too efficiently, like the wolf was once hunted, there would be a danger that he would be exterminated, and thereby 'the source of amusement' be exhausted. Now just as the use of a fox was to be hunted, so the use of a criminal was to be tried. And he had to be given his opportunity to escape from the punishment which might otherwise be due to him.[24] For the lawyers, playing the game was more important than the result.

SINGLE-SEATEDNESS

Bentham would have been critical of the fact that the torture case was heard, and judgement subsequently given, by seven Lords of Appeal, who all more or less say the same thing, at greater or lesser length. The one point of disagreement is over whether to express a new rule of law in a negative or a positive sense: namely, whether it should be said that the Special Immigration Appeals Commission – the court of first instance in this case – should not admit evidence if it has some reason to believe that it has been obtained by torture, or whether it should be said that it should admit evidence if it has no reason to believe that it was obtained by torture. My mind does not possess the requisite subtlety to appreciate the difference between these two propositions, but, as Bentham would have reminded me, incomprehensible points of argument represent a major source of income for lawyers. Bentham recommended that each action undertaken by government should be undertaken by a single, assignable official, no matter whether he belonged to the executive or judiciary. He had two reasons for this: first, the securing of responsibility, in that the public needed to know who to hold accountable; and second, reducing the expense – in the present instance, seven judges cost seven times more in salaries than one judge.[25]

But then again, as Bentham would also have pointed out, it was not a good idea to entrust the task of making law to professional lawyers. English law had been created by lawyers in order to provide 'fee-yielding occasions' for their own benefit. Lots of lawyers and lots of judges and lots of fee-yielding occasions were involved in this torture case – the gravy train rolls on. A few words from the legislature might have settled all doubts. That possibility, however, would only arise where there was a rational system of legislation, which itself would only arise under a properly democratic form of government. Even though Bentham's father was a lawyer (or perhaps because he was a lawyer), and at one time he had himself been destined for the legal profession, and had many friends and 'disciples' who were practising lawyers, he came to dislike lawyers with a passion only equalled by his dislike of priests and aristocrats. Lawyers were liars for hire:

> You are of the Bar – that is to say, the indiscriminate defence of right and wrong, and that for hire, is your occupation: and for the purpose of that occupation, falsehood – self-conscious falsehood, is an instrument which, without stint and without scruple, you are in the continual habit of employing.[26]

And again:

> In this profession [of lawyers], the state of the mind – is it not, to a first view, that of a perfect indifference as between *right* and wrong, for the defence of either of which, as it may happen, a man is hired? To a nearer view, a predilection in favour of *wrong*, as being the most dependent and most profitable customer?[27]

Unlike the medical practitioner, who had an interest in benefiting the community by the cure of his patient, the legal practitioner had an interest in harming the community:

> In medicine the more desperate the case, the greater the glory to the physician who treats it with success and triumphs over the disease. In the practice of the law, the more desperate the case, the greater the glory of the lawyer who treats it with success and triumphs over justice.[28]

The interest of lawyers was in the confusion, not in the clarity, of the law: 'It is . . . the interest of . . . every man of law that, so far as concerns matters of law, men's conceptions of right and wrong should be as confused, as contradictory, as unsettled, and in his hands as pliant as possible'.[29] They were the modern equivalent of the priesthood in ancient Egypt:

> What *priestcraft* with its hieroglyphics was in Egypt, *lawyercraft* with its fictions and technicalities will be seen to be in England: nor were devotees more unmercifully *ridden* by the long-robed cast in Egypt, than they will be found to be in England by men of law.[30]

It is for the lawyers to show whether anything has changed since Bentham's time. On the evidence of this 'landmark' case, we might be justified in thinking that very little had changed.

BENTHAM'S JUSTIFICATION OF TORTURE

Now for the crux of the matter – Bentham's attitude towards torture. In two sequences of manuscript which are thought to have been written around 1780, Bentham justifies the use of torture under certain circumstances. As he did so often, he cautioned against being led astray by sounds – to condemn something because it was called by a name which had unpleasant associations:

> On this subject [of torture] as much as on most others, it behoves us to be on our guard not to be led astray by words. There is no approving it in the lump, without militating against reason and humanity: nor condemning it without falling into absurdities and contradictions.

Bentham defined torture as follows:

> Torture . . . is where a person is made to suffer any violent pain of body in order to compel him to do something or to desist from doing something, which done or desisted from, the penal application is immediately made to cease.[31]

This definition excluded one sense in which torture was commonly used (it was not Bentham's method to try to expound common usage, but rather to 'fix' the meaning of terms). It excluded the notion of torture as the gratuitous or malevolent infliction of pain. Unless some greater benefit accrued from the infliction of pain,

Bentham did not, of course, approve of such an action. Hence the existence of government itself, which, as we have seen on several occasions above, necessarily involved the infliction of pain, was justified insofar as it produced benefits which outweighed the evils. The same was true of the application of torture.

Bentham's definition of torture did include the imposition of pain by some agent of authority in order to extract information or a confession, but it was also wider than this. For instance, it captured the chastisement a child received from a parent when the parent saw the child about to perform an action which could cause the child some significant harm.[32] Take, once again, our example of the boy and the flame of the candle. The boy's father sees him about to put his hand in the flame, but manages to slap his hand, forcing him to withdraw it before he burns himself. The parent has tortured the child, but the child himself has benefited from it – 'it was for his own good', as we say. Bentham also made the point that torture deserved less disapproval than punishment, for two reasons. First, a greater amount of suffering was liable to be inflicted by punishment in order to achieve a purpose which could be achieved by imposing a lesser amount of suffering by means of torture. Second, the point at which torture attained its objective was clear, whereupon it could be brought to an end, whereas it was often not clear how much punishment was needed to achieve its objective. It should be noted that Bentham was adamant that torture should not be used as a punishment.[33]

Bentham put forward a number of conditions under which torture, in a forensic context, had to operate. First, the purpose for which it was applied had to be clear, and it was to cease as soon as that purpose had been attained. In fact, the only purpose for which torture should be employed was to discover information, and not to extract a confession. Second, the action which the prisoner was required to undertake had to be known to be within his power – one had to take the same, if not more stringent, precautions to avoid torturing the innocent as were taken to avoid punishing the innocent. The same level of proof at least was required to subject a person to torture as that required to submit him to punishment. This question should be decided by a judge. If a judge was fit to decide whether a prisoner should be punished, he was fit to decide whether he ought to be tortured. Third, the thing which the prisoner was required to do had to be in the interest of the public.

Here Bentham was prepared to lower the threshold at which torture might be applied in proportion as the benefit to the public was increased – he had in mind cases where 'the safety of the whole state may be endangered for want of that intelligence which it is the object of [the torture] to procure'. On the other hand, torture should not be used in cases where the offence was against the government (persons normally labelled as traitors, libellers or seditious), but only where the offence was against the people (arsonists, murderers, highwaymen and housebreakers). Fourth, there had to be regulations concerning 'the kind and quantity' of torture which it was permissible to employ. The pain inflicted should be of such a kind that it ceased as quickly as possible once the purpose of the torture was accomplished. Fifth, torture should only be used where delay could not be tolerated. Sixth, compensation should be paid to any person wrongly tortured, and any person wrongfully inflicting torture should himself be punished.[34]

An example which Bentham gave where torture might justifiably be used was the following. Two arsonists are arrested for setting fire to a house. One escapes. There is reason to fear that he will set fire to more houses. The prisoner, upon examination, will not say where his friend is likely to be. To obtain the information, the authorities may either promise reward, which mitigates the punishment due to him, or else threaten torture. It may well be the case that the mere threat of torture will produce the desired result without recourse to the infliction of it: 'In countries where torture is absolutely forbidden a malefactor scarce ever betrays his accomplice, for why should he? . . . Establish Torture, and you give him the compleatest of all Excuses, irresistible Necessity.' If a state did not employ torture, together with the threat of torture, criminals would have insufficient motives to inform on their associates – it would be to rely on the 'feeble contingency that a [sense] of religion or an affection for the public interest will prevail against the force of private affection, and the sense of honour'.[35]

Bentham did object to the use to which torture was put in criminal procedure in jurisdictions operating under the civil law, namely, to extract a confession of guilt. If the judge was already satisfied of guilt, there was no need for torture. If he was not satisfied, there was no justification for it. Nor was torture necessary to compel an answer to interrogation. Bentham recommended that the culprit should be advised that if he did not make a satisfactory answer, or if he refused to answer, it would be taken as presumptive evidence of guilt.[36] There should be no 'right to silence'. Interestingly, Lord Bingham links the use of torture to a violation of the right to silence.[37] Bentham did recognize, however, that an 'objection' to torture was the 'great latitude of discretion' which 'must unavoidably be given to somebody with respect to the judging how far the story told by the party interrogated be probable and consistent'.[38] Moreover, where not all laws were good (if all laws were good there could be no 'inconvenience' in compelling a man to give such information as would constitute self-accusation), people had grounds for being unwilling to give information.[39]

All this would seem to suggest that Bentham would have accepted the principle not merely of admitting evidence obtained from those suspected of terrorism by torture, but of the British courts sanctioning its obtainment. However, it is worth adding a few words of caution in relation to the status of the manuscript material on which this account is based. It was not published by Bentham himself, nor by any of his contemporary editors. It consists in two small fragments taken from a massive amount of material written in the 1770s and 1780s for a penal code, itself part of a complete code of laws. Bentham was not recommending the introduction of torture into the Common Law (although he did point out examples where torture, according to his definition, and *contra* the Common Law panegyrists, was in fact used in the Common Law).[40] In order to understand properly what Bentham had in mind, we need to know much more about the context in which he assumed torture would operate. We will have to wait until this material has appeared in authoritative form in *The Collected Works of Jeremy Bentham* in order properly to appreciate Bentham's position. Furthermore, it is not at all clear that Bentham continued to advocate the use of torture. Rather, the presumption is that he ceased to recommend the use of torture when he returned to his work on judicial procedure and evidence after 1803, and when he rewrote his penal code and other codes in the 1820s. Bentham's perspective changed. In the 1770s and 1780s he was writing from the perspective of the legislator. By the 1810s and 1820s he was writing from the perspective of the people. It may be that he had come to think that cross-examination in an inquisitorial setting, where there would be no exclusion of evidence, where the delivery of justice would not suffer from delay, vexation and expense, and where there was a utilitarian code of law in place, would be perfectly adequate to provide the information necessary to deter the commission of offences and to produce rectitude of judicial decision.

LIBERTY AND SECURITY

The torture case represents one aspect of a much wider debate on the relationship, and the perceived opposition, between liberty and security. On one side various government agencies (often referred to as 'the security forces') claim that more regulation is necessary in order to counter the threat from terrorists, while on the other side civil libertarians argue that such regulation will unnecessarily and thus unjustifiably curtail the freedoms of individual citizens. The subtext is that government has an inherent tendency towards authoritarianism. In the United Kingdom, the question of the issuing of identity cards is seen as a test case regarding the limits of legitimate state interference with the individual. Our rulers argue that the issuing of identity cards, giving government agencies the ability to collect and collate more and more information about its citizens, and about the aliens within its borders, will help to identify and nullify the real terrorist threat which we face. Civil libertarians, however, argue that the introduction of identity cards will not achieve its stated purpose, and will undermine individual freedom. However, to couch the debate between liberty and security in terms of the legitimate limits of state interference, and to argue that increase of the one diminishes the other, is, from Bentham's perspective, conceptually flawed.

Bentham would have accepted that, in one sense, liberty and security are diametrically opposed, but not in the more important, substantive sense. For Bentham, security is opposed to liberty in what Isaiah Berlin terms a negative sense, namely the physical capacity or power to perform an action without interference.[41] Liberty is the ability to move the parts of one's body free from restraint or constraint.[42] Such liberty may be used for the benefit of one's self or of others, or to cause harm to one's self or to others.[43] Security is created at the expense of this sort of liberty or physical freedom of action. Security, in the second, substantive sense, is the product of law, and law necessarily imposes coercion – that is restraint or constraint – on some person or persons (unless it is a law repealing an already existing law, in which case it restores the original liberty which existed before the law was enacted). Security is valuable in that it is constitutive of civilized life. Without security, we cannot plan our future, because the necessary conditions for the formation of expectations are lacking. If I am not guaranteed, say, the produce of my labour, I will have no incentive to work. If I am not guaranteed the protection of my property, then I live in constant fear. The creation of security, as noted above, involves the imposition of coercion. Any imposition of coercion is an evil, since it is always more pleasurable to be free to do what I want than to be forced to act in some different way.[44] Yet there are instances, as we have repeatedly seen, in which the necessary evil involved in the imposition of coercion creates greater benefits. Take, for instance, a law which gives security to my person. My liberty is restricted to the extent that I am prohibited from interfering with other people, for instance by hitting them over the head with a baseball bat. Yet the increase in security which I receive from the restriction on every one else's liberty, which means that they are prohibited from hitting me over the head with a baseball bat, is a benefit which far outweighs the evil.

The liberty which the civil libertarians demand in terms of freedom from regulation is not necessarily, from the perspective of either the individual or the community (and, for Bentham, the community is merely an aggregate of individuals), a desirable state of affairs. Liberty in this sense equally includes the liberty to assassinate your neighbour as it does to do unto your neighbour as you would be done by, or merely to leave your neighbour alone. Security, on the other hand, rightly understood, is, from the point of view of both the individual and the community, desirable. As noted above, without security, people cannot live a civilized life. For Bentham, security involves protection for person, property, reputation and condition in life (status). It is not necessarily the case either that more regulation is better or that more regulation is worse. Rather, Bentham's point is that each law should be tested by the criterion of the principle of utility – does it contribute to, or detract from, the happiness or welfare of the individuals who constitute the political community in question? Regulation, to the extent that it creates security, increases opportunity (or freedom); but without regulation, there is no liberty worth having (a fact to which Hobbes alerts us through his description of the state of nature – a state of perfect liberty).[45] The creation of e-bay, for instance, has given people the opportunity to buy and sell goods in a way which had not hitherto been available to them. E-bay is an institution in that it is the product of rules or regulations or laws (the precise relationship between e-bay's 'rules' and 'law' need not detain us, but the 'legal' seems to embrace much more than the enactments of the legislatures and judiciaries of nation-states). The security derived from e-bay's rules has created new opportunities – security is not opposed to what is termed civil liberty, but *is* civil liberty.

To return to identity cards. Bentham would no doubt have approved of the introduction of identity cards – not because he was an authoritarian, with a wish to extend the control of the state over more and more aspects of the lives of individuals, but because he wanted to expand people's opportunities and freedoms. Indeed, Bentham himself advocated the introduction of a somewhat crude, but fraud-proof, type of 'personal identity mark' – namely, the tattoo.[46] Everyone should bear a tattoo – including the monarch. You could then be confident that the person with whom you were dealing was the person he claimed to be.[47]

Panopticon has been represented by civil libertarians (and to widen the argument, utilitarianism has been represented by theorists of human rights) as a violation of human rights and as an affront to human dignity. Benthamism does indeed stand as a challenge to the course taken by rights-based liberalism. From Bentham's point of view, the notions of human rights and of human dignity are bound up with theology, and lack any ontological basis. It is only when we recognize that the modern state, together with the federal and confederal institutions which it has spawned, is best placed on a utilitarian basis, that we will be able to work with it – rather than against it, as human rights advocates and supporters do – in order to promote the happiness of the whole community.

POST-OBIT POSTSCRIPT

Bentham died on 6 July 1832. In his will he directed that his body should be dissected for the benefit of medical students.[48] Once the anatomical lectures had been completed, he further directed that his skeleton should 'be put together in such manner as that the whole figure may be seated in a Chair usually occupied by me when living in the attitude in which I am sitting when engaged in thought'. The skeleton was to be clothed in one of his black suits, and placed in 'an appropriate box or case'. This operation was carried out by Bentham's friend and surgeon Thomas Southwood Smith, who created Bentham's 'auto-icon' or self-image, consisting of his skeleton and clothes, with the addition of a wax head.[49] Smith gave the auto-icon a home for nearly 20 years, but when he moved to a smaller house, he decided not to take his non-paying lodger with him. He donated it to University College, London, where it remains (no pun intended) today.

What did Bentham hope to achieve with his auto-icon? In a short, satirical essay titled 'Auto-Icon; or, Of the Farther Uses of the Dead to the Living',[50] he envisaged a whole range of uses for auto-icons. They could, for instance, take part in theatrical performances, and would be particularly impressive if they were animated – a small boy could be hidden behind each auto-icon, and by suitable mechanical contrivances move its arms and head. A country gentleman who had 'rows of trees leading to his dwelling' might place 'the Auto-Icons of his family' between the trees.[51] Auto-icons would have religious uses, for instance, becoming the centres of pilgrimage. Bentham imagined that his own auto-icon, surrounded by shelves containing his manuscripts, might become one such centre. The pilgrimage would be made by 'the votaries of the greatest-happiness principle'.[52] Auto-iconization would save the expense of funeral rites, and particularly benefit the poor, who would no longer feel constrained to sacrifice their 'bodily comfort and enjoyment' in order to provide an 'ostentatious funeral' for their relatives. If the body was not auto-iconized, it could be inexpensively disposed of in a pit of lime.[53]

What, then, does the auto-icon represent? Perhaps this is the most perplexing question of all. Is it an act of vanity? Is it a publicity stunt? Is it a joke? Is it an attempt to mock religion? Is it the first post-modern piece of art? You are welcome to come to London to pay your respects to Mr Bentham, and decide for yourself.

FURTHER READING

The website of the Bentham Project, which is producing the new authoritative edition of *The Collected Works of Jeremy Bentham*, provides an excellent resource for the study of Bentham (www. ucl.ac.uk/Bentham-Project (last accessed on 29 Oct. 2008)), and includes a comprehensive and up-to-date bibliography. You will also find an on-line version of the *Bentham Newsletter*, 12 vols, 1978–88, together with the electronic *Journal of Bentham Studies* (instituted 1997). The *Bentham Newsletter* was succeeded by the journal *Utilitas*, published from 1989 by Oxford University Press, from 1995 by Edinburgh University Press, and from 2004 by Cambridge University Press. *Utilitas* is the major academic journal catering for scholars with an interest in utilitarian studies generally, and contains many important articles on Bentham.

PRIMARY SOURCES

Wherever possible, Bentham should be read in the new *Collected Works* (General Editors J. H. Burns (1961–79); J. R. Dinwiddy (1979–83); F. Rosen (1983–95); F. Rosen and P. Schofield (1995–2003); P. Schofield (2003–)). Bentham's *Correspondence* (various editors) has now reached 12 volumes (vols I–V London: Athlone, vols. VI–XII Oxford: Clarendon Press), covering the years from Bentham's earliest recorded letter (aged 3) in 1752 to June 1828. The correspondence is extremely valuable for the insights it gives into Bentham's personality, his friends and connections, the composition of his works, and his preoccupations at any given period.

The most accessible starting-point for Bentham's thought is *A Fragment on Government* (first published in 1776), which appears in Bentham, J. (1977), *A Comment on the Commentaries and A*

Fragment on Government. J. H. Burns and H. L. A. Hart (eds), London: Athlone Press. The Burns and Hart edition of *A Fragment on Government* is available in Cambridge Texts in the History of Political Thought, with an introduction by R. Harrison. While *A Fragment on Government* does not contain an exposition of the principle of utility, it does introduce a number of important themes which Bentham developed in more detail over the course of his career. The most famous account of Bentham's utilitarianism, together with his theory of punishment, is found in Bentham, J. (1970a), *An Introduction to the Principles of Morals and Legislation*. J. H. Burns and H. L. A. Hart (eds), London: Athlone Press (also available as an Oxford University Press paperback, with an introduction by F. Rosen and a classic essay by Hart). For Bentham's more mature reflection on ethics and the principle of utility see Bentham, J. (1983c), *Deontology together with A Table of the Springs of Action and Article on Utilitarianism*. A. Goldworth (ed.), Oxford: Clarendon Press.

Bentham's theory of law is expounded in Bentham, J. (1970b), *Of Laws in General*. H. L. A. Hart (ed.), London: Athlone Press (but soon to be superseded by a new edition titled *Of the Limits of the Penal Branch of Jurisprudence*), while his later thinking on codification is found in Bentham, J. (1998), *'Legislator of the World': Writings on Codification, Law, and Education*. P. Schofield and J. Harris (eds), Oxford: Clarendon Press. Bentham's highly original treatment of the best mode of procedure to be adopted in legislative assemblies appears in Bentham, J. (1999), *Political Tactics*. M. James, C. Blamires and C. Pease-Watkin (eds), Oxford: Clarendon Press. Bentham's social theory can be approached through Bentham, J. (2001), *Writings on the Poor Laws: Vol. I*. M. Quinn (ed.), Oxford: Clarendon Press; and Bentham, J. (2009) *Writings on the Poor Laws: Vol. II*. M. Quinn (ed.), Oxford: Clarendon Press.

For Bentham's political thought at the time of the French Revolution see Bentham, J. (2002), *Rights, Representation, and Reform: Nonsense upon Stilts and other writings on the French Revolution*. P. Schofield, C. Pease-Watkin and C. Blamires (eds), Oxford: Clarendon Press. His later democratic thought can be approached through a series of volumes: Bentham, J. (1983a), *Constitutional Code: Vol. I*. F. Rosen and J. H. Burns (eds), Oxford: Clarendon Press; Bentham, J. (1989b), *First Principles preparatory to Constitutional Code*. P. Schofield (ed.), Oxford: Clarendon Press;

Bentham, J. (1990), *Securities against Misrule and other Constitutional Writings for Tripoli and Greece*. P. Schofield (ed.), Oxford: Clarendon Press; Bentham, J. (1993), *Official Aptitude Maximized; Expense Minimized*. P. Schofield (ed.), Oxford: Clarendon Press; and Bentham, J. (1995), *Colonies, Commerce, and Constitutional Law: Rid Yourselves of Ultramaria and Other Writings on Spain and Spanish America*. Oxford: Clarendon Press. For Bentham's ideas on education see Bentham, J. (1983b), *Chrestomathia*. M. J. Smith and W. H. Burston (eds), Oxford: Clarendon Press, which is also valuable for his views on logic and language.

Where texts are not available in the *Collected Works*, we must fall back on the 11 volume *Works* edited 'under the superintendence of' John Bowring (known as the Bowring edition, or simply as Bowring) issued in parts between 1838 and 1843, and then published as a complete set (Bentham, J. (1843), *The Works of Jeremy Bentham*. J. Bowring (ed.), 11 vols, Edinburgh: William Tait). The Bowring edition is problematic because of the varying status of the works it contains: some are straightforward reprints of works published by Bentham himself; some were edited after Bentham's death by his 'disciples', and are of uneven quality; and others are English translations of the French translations of Bentham's manuscripts first published by Étienne Dumont (see Chapter One, p. 14 above). Still valuable, at least until replaced by the new edition of Bentham's economic writings which is currently in progress, is Bentham, J. (1952–4), *Jeremy Bentham's Economic Writings*. W. Stark (ed.), 3 vols, London: George Allen and Unwin.

For 'Of Ontology', an important essay from Bentham's writings on logic and language, see the bilingual edition Bentham, J. (1997), *De l'ontologie et autres textes sur les fictions*. P. Schofield, J. P. Cléro and C. Laval (eds), Paris: Éditions du Seuil; and for a selection of writings on religion (omitted from Bowring) see Crimmins, J. E. (1998), *Utilitarians and Religion*. Bristol: Thoemmes, pp. 275–414.

SECONDARY SOURCES

Many critical essays on Bentham have been collected together in Parekh, B. (1993), *Jeremy Bentham: Critical Assessments*. 4 vols, London: Routledge; and in Postema, G. J. (2002), *Bentham: Moral, Political, and Legal Philosophy*. 2 vols, Aldershot: Dartmouth. A collection which reproduces a number of key contributions to a selection of recent debates in Bentham studies is Rosen, F. (2007), *Jeremy Bentham*. Aldershot: Ashgate.

Introducing Bentham

The best introduction to Bentham's life remains Dinwiddy, J. R. (1989), *Bentham*. Oxford: Oxford University Press, reprinted in Dinwiddy, J. (2003), *Bentham: Selected Writings of John Dinwiddy*. W. Twining (ed.), Stanford, CA: Stanford University Press. Frederick Rosen's article on Bentham for the *Oxford Dictionary of National Biography* is also an excellent starting-point. Still interesting is Steintrager, J. (1977), *Bentham*. Ithaca, NY: Cornell University Press, while Christie, I. R. (1993), *The Benthams in Russia 1780–1791*. Oxford: Berg, deals in detail with Samuel Bentham's activities in Russia in the 1780s and Jeremy's journey to visit him. An important general work is Harrison, R. (1983), *Bentham*. London: Routledge & Kegan Paul; while Halévy, E. (1928), *The Growth of Philosophic Radicalism*. M. Morris (trans.), London: Faber & Faber, contains the classic exposition of Bentham's thought. Written before the appearance of the new edition of Bentham's writings, Baumgardt, D. (1952), *Bentham and the Ethics of Today*. Princeton, NJ: Princeton University Press contains many impressive insights. For more discursive introductions to Bentham scholarship see Twining, W. (1989), 'Reading Bentham'. *Proceedings of the British Academy*, 85, 97–141; and Twining, W. (1998), 'Imagining Bentham: a celebration'. *Current Legal Problems*, 51, 1–36. For excellent studies which place Bentham's thought against a wider historical background see Rosen, F. (1992), *Bentham, Byron and Greece: Constitutionalism, Nationalism, and Early Liberal Political Thought*. Oxford: Clarendon Press; Rosen F. (2003), *Classical Utilitarianism from Hume to Mill*. London: Routledge; and Engelmann, S. G. (2003), *Imagining Interest in Political Thought: Origins of Economic Rationality*. Durham, NC: Duke University Press.

Utility

The aspect of Bentham's thought which attracts most interest is his utilitarianism – almost all the major books on Bentham deal with this aspect of his thought: see, for instance, Hart, H. L. A. (1983), *Essays on Bentham: Jurisprudence and Political Theory*. Oxford:

Clarendon Press, pp. 79–104; Kelly, P. J. (1990), *Utilitarianism and Distributive Justice: Jeremy Bentham and the Civil Law*. Oxford: Clarendon Press, pp. 14–70; and Harrison, *Bentham*, pp. 167–94. A controversial interpretation of *An Introduction to the Principles of Morals and Legislation* by Lyons, D. (1973, revised edn 1991), *In the Interest of the Governed: A Study in Bentham's Philosophy of Utility and Law*. Oxford: Clarendon Press, prompted a convincing response in Dinwiddy, J. R. (1982), 'Bentham on private ethics and the principle of utility'. *Revue Internationale de Philosophie*, 36, 278–300. For my 'naturalistic' interpretation of Bentham's utilitarianism see Schofield, P. (2006), *Utility and Democracy: The Political Thought of Jeremy Bentham*. Oxford: Oxford University Press, pp. 28–50. Important articles which deal with various aspects of the principle of utility are as follows: Goldworth, A. (1969), 'The meaning of Bentham's greatest happiness principle'. *History of Philosophy*, 7, 315–21; Shackleton, R. (1972), 'The greatest happiness of the greatest number: the history of Bentham's phrase'. *Studies on Voltaire and the Eighteenth Century*, 90, 1461–82; Rosen, F. (1998), 'Individual sacrifice and the greatest happiness: Bentham on utility and rights'. *Utilitas*, 10 (2), 129–43, and restated in Rosen, *Classical Utilitarianism*, pp. 220–31 (in response see Postema, G. J. (1998), 'Bentham's equality-sensitive utilitarianism'. *Utilitas*, 10 (2), 144–58); Postema, G. J. (2006), 'Interests, universal and particular: Bentham's utilitarian theory of value'. *Utilitas*, 18 (2), 109–33; and Warke, T. (2000), 'Multi-dimensional utility and the index number problem: Jeremy Bentham, J. S. Mill, and qualitative hedonism'. *Utilitas*, 12 (2), 176–203.

Closely related to the principle of utility are Bentham's four sub-ends of utility, namely, subsistence, abundance, security and equality: see Kelly, *Utilitarianism and Distributive Justice*; Postema, G. J. (1986). *Bentham and the Common Law Tradition*. Oxford: Clarendon Press; Quinn, M. (2008), 'A failure to reconcile the irreconcilable? Security, subsistence and equality in Bentham's writings on the civil code and on the poor laws'. *History of Political Thought*, 29 (2), 320–43; and Engelmann, *Imagining Interest*, pp. 48–76.

Legal Theory

There is an excellent literature on Bentham's legal theory. For historical accounts of Bentham's legal thought see Lieberman, D.

(1989), *The Province of Legislation Determined: Legal Theory in Eighteenth-Century Britain*. Cambridge: Cambridge University Press, pp. 217–90; and Lobban, M. (1991), *The Common Law and English Jurisprudence 1760–1850*. Oxford: Clarendon Press, pp. 116–222. For a philosophical reconstruction of Bentham's legal positivism see Postema, *Bentham and the Common Law Tradition*, pp. 218–62. For the relationship between utility, liberty and law in Bentham's thought see Long, D. G. (1977), *Bentham on Liberty: Jeremy Bentham's Idea of Liberty in relation to his Utilitarianism*. Toronto: University of Toronto Press. The view that Bentham can be characterized as a legal positivist as that term is understood by Hart is questioned in Schofield, P. (2003), 'Jeremy Bentham, the principle of utility, and legal positivism'. *Current Legal Problems*, 56, 1–39. On the more specific topic of Bentham's theory of sovereignty see Hart, *Essays on Bentham*, pp. 105–26, 194–268; Burns, J. H. (1993), 'Nature and natural authority in Bentham'. *Utilitas*, 5 (2), 209–19; James, M. H. (1973), 'Bentham on the individuation of laws', in M. H. James (ed.), *Bentham and Legal Theory*, pp. 91–116 (reprinted from *Northern Ireland Legal Quarterly*, 24 (3)); and Burns, J. H. (1973), 'Bentham on sovereignty: an exploration', in ibid., pp. 133–50. For a challenging but rewarding account of Bentham's theory of sovereignty see Ben Dor, O. (2000), *Constitutional Limits and the Public Sphere: A Critical Study of Bentham's Constitutionalism*. Oxford: Hart.

Natural Rights

Bentham's attack on natural rights has generated an impressive literature: see Hart, *Essays on Bentham*, pp. 53–104; Twining, W. L. (1975), 'The contemporary significance of Bentham's Anarchical Fallacies'. *Archiv für Rechts– und Sozialphilosophie*, 61 (3), 325–56; Waldron, J. (ed.) (1987), *Nonsense upon Stilts: Bentham, Burke, and Marx on the Rights of Man*. London: Methuen, pp. 29–76; Bedau, H. A. (2000), ' "Anarchical Fallacies": Bentham's attack on human rights'. *Human Rights Quarterly*, 22 (1), 261–79; Lacey, N. (1998), 'Bentham as proto-feminist? or an ahistorical fantasy on "Anarchical Fallacies" '. *Current Legal Problems*, 51, 441–66; Postema, G. J. (1989), 'In defence of "French nonsense": fundamental rights in constitutional jurisprudence', in N. MacCormick and Z. Bankowski (eds), *Enlightenment, Rights and Revolution: Essays in*

Legal and Social Philosophy. Aberdeen: Aberdeen University Press, pp. 107–33; and Schofield, P. (2003), 'Jeremy Bentham's "Nonsense upon Stilts"'. *Utilitas*, 15 (1), 1–26.

Real and Fictitious Entities

Bentham's distinction between real and fictitious entities, often referred to as his theory of fictions, deserves much more attention than it has hitherto received, both from Bentham scholars and historians of philosophy more generally. The most detailed account is Harrison, *Bentham*, pp. 24–105, but also valuable are Hart, *Essays on Bentham*, pp. 42–4, 128–31; Schofield, *Utility and Democracy*, pp. 1–27; and Postema, G. (1983), 'Fact, fictions and law: Bentham on the foundations of evidence', in W. L. Twining, ed., *Facts in Law*. Wiesbaden: Franz Steiner, pp. 37–64. For a post-modern twist see Jackson, B. S. (1998), 'Bentham, truth and the semiotics of law'. *Current Legal Problems*, 51, 493–531.

Punishment and Panopticon

On Bentham's theory of punishment see Bedau, H. A. (1983), 'Bentham's utilitarian critique of the death penalty'. *The Journal of Criminal Law and Criminology*, 74 (3), 1033–65; Draper, A. (2002), 'An introduction to Jeremy Bentham's theory of punishment'. *Journal of Bentham Studies*, 5 (www.ucl.ac.uk/Bentham-Project/journal/adpunt.htm (last accessed on 29 Oct. 2008)); and Rosen, *Classical Utilitarianism*, pp. 209–19. Closely related to the writings on punishment are Bentham's writings on the panopticon prison. The most detailed (and surprisingly entertaining) account is Semple, J. E. (1993), *Bentham's Prison: A Study of the Panopticon Penitentiary*. Oxford: Clarendon Press, although the most influential has been Foucault, M. (1977), *Discipline and Punish: The Birth of the Prison*. A. Sheridan (trans.), London: Allen Lane, esp. pp. 195–228. The tradition of criticism of panopticon is well represented by Himmelfarb, G. (1968), *Victorian Minds*. London: Weidenfeld and Nicolson, pp. 32–81. Semple has responded to Himmelfarb and Foucault respectively in Semple, J. E. (1987), 'Bentham's haunted house'. *Bentham Newsletter*, 11, 35–44, and Semple, J. E. (1992), 'Foucault and Bentham: a defence of panopticism'. *Utilitas*, 4 (1), 105–20. Panopticon as part of a story of the invention of bureaucracy

is the theme of Hume, L. J. (1981), *Bentham and Bureaucracy.*
Cambridge: Cambridge University Press, pp. 110–64.

Poverty

Almost as controversial as the panopticon prison has been
Bentham's views on the poor laws. For a sympathetic account see
Roberts, W. (1979), 'Bentham's Poor Law Proposals'. *Bentham
Newsletter*, 3, 28–45, and for strident critiques see Himmelfarb, G.
(1970), 'Bentham's utopia: the National Charity Company'. *Journal
of British Studies*, 10 (1), 80–125; and Bahmueller, C. (1981), *The
National Charity Company: Jeremy Bentham's Silent Revolution.*
Berkeley, CA: University of California Press. A balanced approach
is adopted by Quinn, M. (1994), 'Jeremy Bentham on the relief of
indigence: an exercise in applied philosophy'. *Utilitas*, 6 (1), 81–96.
Bentham's views on this and other aspects of social policy are
considered in the excellent Boralevi, L. C. (1984), *Bentham and
the Oppressed*. Berlin: Walter de Gruyter. For the historical background see Poynter, J. R. (1969), *Society and Pauperism: English
Ideas on Poor Relief 1795–1834*. London: Routledge & Kegan Paul.

Political Thought

For the debate on Bentham's political thought at the time of the
French Revolution see Burns, J. H. (1966), 'Bentham and the French
Revolution'. *Transactions of the Royal Historical Society*, 5th Series,
16, 95–114, responding to an influential, but misleading, hypothesis
put forward by Mack, M. P. (1962), *Jeremy Bentham: An Odyssey
of Ideas 1748–1792*. London: Heinemann. Other contributions to
the debate include James, M. H. (1986) 'Bentham's democratic theory at the time of the French Revolution'. *Bentham Newsletter*, 10,
5–16; and Long, D. G. (1988), 'Censorial jurisprudence and political radicalism: a reconsideration of the early Bentham'. *Bentham
Newsletter*, 12, 4–23. For Bentham's transition to political democracy see Dinwiddy, J. R. (1975), 'Bentham's transition to political
radicalism, 1809–10'. *Journal of the History of Ideas*, 36 (4), 683–700;
Crimmins, J. E. (1994), 'Bentham's political radicalism reexamined'.
Journal of the History of Ideas, 55 (2), 259–81; and Rosen, F. (2007),
'Jeremy Bentham's radicalism', in G. Burgess and M. Festenstein
(eds), *English Radicalism 1550–1850*. Cambridge: Cambridge

University Press, pp. 217–40. For a superb essay which captures the movement from Bentham's earlier to his later political thought see Burns, J. H. (1984), 'Jeremy Bentham: from radical Enlightenment to philosophical radicalism'. *Bentham Newsletter*, 8, 4–14. I have tried to provide a framework for understanding the development of Bentham's political thought, in which his discovery of sinister interests plays a central role, in Schofield, *Utility and Democracy*.

For Bentham's constitutional writings, which dominated the final decade of his life, see Rosen, F. (1983), *Jeremy Bentham and Representative Democracy: A Study of the Constitutional Code*. Oxford: Clarendon Press, which can be supplemented with Hume, *Bentham and Bureaucracy*, pp. 209–58, and Harrison, *Bentham*, pp. 167–262. For an excellent study of Bentham's constitutional thought in the context of his science of legislation see Lieberman, D. (2000), 'Economy and polity in Bentham's science of legislation', in S. Collini, R. Whatmore and B. Young (eds), *Economy, Polity, and Society: British Intellectual History 1750–1950*. Cambridge: Cambridge University Press, pp. 107–34.

Benthamism

For the reception of Bentham's ideas, particularly in relation to the codification of the law, see Dinwiddy, J. R. (1984), 'Bentham and the early nineteenth century'. *Bentham Newsletter*, 8, 15–33; Dinwiddy, J. R. (1984), 'Early nineteenth-century reactions to Benthamism'. *Transactions of the Royal Historical Society*, 5th series, 34, 47–69; and Schofield, P. (1998), 'Jeremy Bentham: legislator of the world'. *Current Legal Problems*, 51, 115–47. For Dumont's role in the transmission of Bentham's ideas see Blamires, C. (2008), *The French Revolution and the Creation of Benthamism*. Basingstoke: Palgrave Macmillan.

Miscellaneous

A selection of important books and essays on particular aspects of Bentham's thought is as follows: Rosen, F. (2005), 'Jeremy Bentham on slavery and the slave trade', in B. Schultz and G. Varouxakis (eds), *Utilitarianism and Empire*. Lanham, MD: Lexington Books, pp. 33–56; J. Pitts, 'Legislator of the world? A rereading of Bentham on colonies'. *Political Theory*, 31 (2), 200–34; Twining, W. (1985),

Theories of Evidence: Bentham and Wigmore. London: Weidenfeld & Nicolson; Conway, S. (1989), 'Bentham on peace and war'. *Utilitas,* 1 (1), 82–101; and Conway, S. (1990), 'Bentham and the nineteenth-century revolution in government', in R. Bellamy (ed.), *Victorian Liberalism: Nineteenth-Century Political Thought and Practice.* London: Routledge, pp. 71–80.

Religion

A pioneering essay on Bentham's religious thought is Steintrager, J. (1980), 'Language and politics: Bentham on religion'. *Bentham Newsletter,* 4, 4–20. Steintrager's insights are developed in detail in Crimmins, J. E. (1990), *Secular Utilitarianism: Social Science and the Critique of Religion in the Thought of Jeremy Bentham.* Oxford: Clarendon Press, whose approach is criticized in Schofield, P. (1999), 'Political and religious radicalism in the thought of Jeremy Bentham'. *History of Political Thought,* 20 (2), 272–91, itself the subject of criticism in Crimmins, J. E. (2001), 'Bentham's religious radicalism revisited: a response to Schofield'. *History of Political Thought,* 22 (3), 494–500. Bentham's religious ideas are related to contemporary theological debates in McKown, D. B. (2004), *Behold the Antichrist: Bentham on Religion.* Amherst, NY: Prometheus Books.

Centre Bentham

There is a burgeoning literature on Bentham in French, associated with the *Centre Bentham* based in Paris (http://bentham.free.fr/index. html (last accessed on 29 Oct. 2008)), which is producing modern French translations of Bentham's works and editing *Revue d'Etudes Benthamiennes.* Recent monographs from scholars associated with the *Centre* include Sigot, N. (2001), *Bentham et l'économie: une histoire d'utilité,* Paris: Economica; Tusseau, G. (2001), *Jeremy Bentham et le droit constitutionnel: une approche de l'utilitarisme juridique.* Paris: L'Harmattan; Brunon-Ernst, A. (2007), *Le panoptique des pauvres: Jeremy Bentham et la réforme de l'assistance en Angleterre.* Paris: Presses Sorbonne Nouvelle; and de Champs, E. (2008), *La déontologie politique: ou la pensée constitutionelle de Jeremy Bentham.* Genève: Librairie Droz.

NOTES

CHAPTER ONE: WHO WAS JEREMY BENTHAM?

1. The details of Bentham's life which are not separately referenced are taken from the several Introductions to the 12 volumes of Bentham's correspondence published in the new authoritative edition of *The Collected Works of Jeremy Bentham*, regarding which see Chapter 2, pp. 24–30, 42–3 below.
2. Bentham, J. (1843), *The Works of Jeremy Bentham*. J. Bowring (ed.), 11 vols, Edinburgh: William Tait, x. 21.
3. Bentham, J. (1818), *Church-of-Englandism and its Catechism Examined*. London: Effingham Wilson, Preface, pp. xi–xii.
4. Bowring, x. 22–4.
5. Ibid., x. 21.
6. Ibid., x. 10–11, 21–2.
7. Bentham, *Church-of-Englandism*. Preface, p. xxi.
8. See, for instance, Steintrager, J. (1980), 'Language and politics: Bentham on religion'. *Bentham Newsletter*, 4, 4–20; and Crimmins, J. E. (1990), *Secular Utilitarianism: Social Science and the Critique of Religion in the Thought of Jeremy Bentham*. Oxford: Clarendon Press, pp. 282–92.
9. Bentham, J. (1989a), *The Correspondence of Jeremy Bentham: Vol. IX*. S. Conway (ed.), Oxford: Clarendon Press, pp. 418–19.
10. See Bentham, J. (1977), *A Comment on the Commentaries and A Fragment on Government*. J. H. Burns and H. L. A. Hart (eds), London: Athlone Press, p. 399.
11. Blackstone, W. (1765–9), *Commentaries on the Laws of England*. 4 vols, Oxford: Clarendon Press.
12. Burns, J. H. (1989), 'Bentham and Blackstone: a lifetime's dialectic'. *Utilitas*, 1 (1), 22–40.
13. Bowring, x. 51.
14. Ibid., x. 54.
15. See pp. 44–69 below.
16. Bowring, x. 27.
17. Bentham, J. (1970a), *An Introduction to the Principles of Morals and Legislation*. J. H. Burns and H. L. A. Hart (eds), London: Athlone Press.

18. Hart, H. L. A. (1983), *Essays in Jurisprudence and Philosophy*. Oxford: Clarendon Press, pp. 49–87.
19. The most famous and influential of these pamphlets was [Lind, J.] (1775), *Remarks on the Principal Acts of the Thirteenth Parliament of Great Britain. Vol. I. Containing Remarks on the Acts relating to the Colonies. With a Plan of Reconciliation*. London: T. Payne.
20. See Rudan, P. (2007), 'Dalla costituzione al governo. Jeremy Bentham e le Americhe'. University of Bologna Ph.D.
21. See pp. 44–69 below.
22. Draper, A. J. (2000), 'Cesare Beccaria's influence on English discussions of punishment, 1764–1789'. *History of European Ideas*, 26 (3), 177–99.
23. *IPML*, pp. 165–86.
24. Ibid., pp. 187–91, 223–4.
25. See ibid., pp. 158–64 for Bentham's discussion of 'cases unmeet [i.e. unsuitable] for punishment'.
26. Bentham, J. (1970b), *Of Laws in General*. H. L. A. Hart (ed.), London: Athlone Press. For further discussion of this text see Chapter 2, pp. 39–42 below.
27. Lieberman, D. (1989), *The Province of Legislation Determined: Legal Theory in Eighteenth-Century Britain*. Cambridge: Cambridge University Press, pp. 257–76.
28. The most accessible of Bentham's works on this subject is 'Codification Proposal', which first appeared in 1822: see Bentham, J. (1998), *'Legislator of the World': Writings on Codification, Law, and Education*. P. Schofield and J. Harris (eds), Oxford: Clarendon Press, pp. 243–97.
29. The role of the civil law in promoting these sub-ends is given detailed treatment in Kelly, P. J. (1990), *Utilitarianism and Distributive Justice: Jeremy Bentham and the Civil Law*. Oxford: Clarendon Press.
30. Bentham, *'Legislator of the World'*, pp. 122 n. a, 194–239, 245–57.
31. See pp. 137–52 below.
32. Bentham, *'Legislator of the World'*, p. 168.
33. Ibid., pp. 128–36. For the relationship between rules, expectations, security and utility in Bentham's legal theory see Postema, G. J. (1986). *Bentham and the Common Law Tradition*. Oxford, Clarendon Press, pp. 147–90.
34. Bowring, x. 66.
35. The contrast between the political thought of Bentham in the eighteenth and in the nineteenth centuries is the subject of Burns, J. H. (1984), 'Jeremy Bentham: from radical Enlightenment to philosophical radicalism'. *Bentham Newsletter*, 8, 4–14.
36. See Dinwiddy, J. R. (1975), 'Bentham's transition to political radicalism, 1809–10'. *Journal of the History of Ideas*, 36 (4), 683–700, for a consideration of the various factors which might have influenced Bentham at this time.
37. See Mack, M. P. (1962), *Jeremy Bentham: An Odyssey of Ideas 1748–1792*. London: Heinemann, pp. 407–43.
38. Burns, J. H. (1966), 'Bentham and the French Revolution'. *Transactions of the Royal Historical Society*, 5th Series, 16, 95–114.

39. See Bentham, J. (2002), *Rights, Representation, and Reform: Nonsense upon Stilts and other writings on the French Revolution*. P. Schofield, C. Pease-Watkin and C. Blamires (eds), Oxford: Clarendon Press.
40. Schofield, P. (2006), *Utility and Democracy: The Political Thought of Jeremy Bentham*. Oxford: Oxford University Press, pp. 78–108.
41. See Burns, 'Bentham and the French Revolution', 110–12.
42. See pp. 70–93 below.
43. See Semple, J. E. (1993), *Bentham's Prison: A Study of the Panopticon Penitentiary*. Oxford: Clarendon Press, pp. 254–82.
44. The phrase first appears in print in Bentham, J. (1798), 'Outline of a work entitled Pauper Management Improved'. *Annals of Agriculture*, 30 (173), 482 (reprinted in Bowring, viii. 415).
45. Schofield, *Utility and Democracy*, pp. 109–70.
46. Bentham collected together his correspondence with heads of state and other politicians in the Testimonials attached to 'Codification Proposal': see Bentham, *'Legislator of the World'*, pp. 298–384.
47. See ibid., pp. 335–6.
48. Bentham, J. (1995a), *Colonies, Commerce, and Constitutional Law: Rid Yourselves of Ultramaria and other writings on Spain and Spanish America*. Oxford: Clarendon Press.
49. Bentham, J. (1990). *Securities against Misrule and other Constitutional Writings for Tripoli and Greece*. P. Schofield (ed.), Oxford: Clarendon Press.
50. See, for instance, Gallo, K. (2006), *The Struggle for an Enlightened Republic: Buenos Aires and Rivadavia*. London: Institute for the Study of the Americas, pp. 26–45; and Uribe, J. J. (2001), *El pensamiento colombiano en el siglo XIX (Obras Completas de Jaime Jaramillo Uribe)*, Bogotá: Alfomega, pp. 117–25.
51. See *IPML*, p. 296 n. x.
52. See Valle to Bentham, *c.* 1826, reproduced in Bentham, *'Legislator of the World'*, pp. 370–1: 'Sus obras le dan el titulo glorioso de legislador del mundo.' For the portrait see Fuller, C. (ed.), (1998), *The Old Radical: Representations of Jeremy Bentham*. London: University College London, pp. 56–7.
53. Shelburne had been at the head of the British ministry in 1782–3.
54. See Norris, J. (1963), *Shelburne and Reform*. London: Macmillan, pp. 141–3, 279–80.
55. See Blamires, C. (2008), *The French Revolution and the Creation of Benthamism*. Basingstoke: Palgrave Macmillan.
56. Bentham Papers, University College London library, Box xxiv, fo 188v (18 November 1821).
57. Bentham, J. (1989b), *First Principles preparatory to Constitutional Code*. P. Schofield (ed.), Oxford: Clarendon Press, pp. 179–80.
58. See Bentham to Sir Frederick Morton Eden, 4 September 1802, in Bentham, J. (1988), *The Correspondence of Jeremy Bentham: Vol. VII*. J. R. Dinwiddy (ed.), Oxford: Clarendon Press, p. 124.
59. Bowring, xi. 33, 80.
60. *IPML*, p. 11.

61. See Bentham, '*Legislator of the World*', pp. 322–3 n. 8.
62. For earlier appreciations of Bentham see, for instance, Ogden, C. K. (1932), *Jeremy Bentham, 1832–2032*. London: Kegan Paul, Trench, Trubner & Co.; Baumgardt, D. (1952), *Bentham and the Ethics of Today*. Princeton: Princeton University Press, pp. 3–14; and Hart, H. L. A. (1983), *Essays on Bentham: Jurisprudence and Political Theory*. Oxford: Clarendon Press, pp. 1–20.
63. See Chapter 3, pp. 58–60 below.
64. Warke, T. (2000), 'Mathematical fitness in the evolution of the utility concept from Bentham to Jevons to Marshall'. *Journal of the History of Economic Thought*, 22 (1), 3–27.
65. See Hart, *Essays on Bentham*; and Postema, *Bentham and the Common Law Tradition*.
66. The essay appears in authoritative form, under its proper title, for the first time in Bentham, *Rights, Representation, and Reform*, pp. 318–401. More generally see Waldron, J. (ed.) (1987), *Nonsense upon Stilts: Bentham, Burke, and Marx on the Rights of Man*. London: Methuen.
67. See Twining, W. (1985), *Theories of Evidence: Bentham and Wigmore*. London: Weidenfeld & Nicolson.
68. Draper, A. J. (1987), 'Jeremy Bentham's Theory of Punishment'. University of London Ph.D.
69. See 'The Rationale of Reward', in Bowring, ii. 189–266.
70. See Bentham, *Rights, Representation, and Reform*, pp. 67–78, 246–9.
71. See Bentham, J. (1983a), *Constitutional Code: Vol. I*. F. Rosen and J. H. Burns (eds), Oxford: Clarendon Press; and Rosen, F. (1983a), *Jeremy Bentham and Representative Democracy: A Study of the Constitutional Code*. Oxford: Clarendon Press.
72. Bentham, J. (1999), *Political Tactics*. M. James, C. Blamires and C. Pease-Watkin (eds), Oxford: Clarendon Press.
73. Foucault, M. (1977), *Discipline and Punish: The Birth of the Prison*. A. Sheridan (trans.), London: Allen Lane.
74. See Ben Dor, O. (2000), *Constitutional Limits and the Public Sphere: A Critical Study of Bentham's Constitutionalism*. Oxford: Hart; and Engelmann, S. G. (2001), 'Imagining interest'. *Utilitas*, 13 (3), 289–322.
75. Foucault, M. (1994), *Dits et écrits, 1954–1988*. D. Defert, F. Ewald and J. Lagrange (eds), 4 vols, Paris: Gallimard, ii. 594.
76. See 'Principles of International Law', in Bowring, ii. 535–60; and Hoogensen, G. (2005), *International Relations, Security and Jeremy Bentham*, London: Routledge.
77. See, for instance, Bentham, *Colonies, Commerce, and Constitutional Law*; and Pitts, J. (2005), *A Turn to Empire: The Rise of Imperial Liberalism in Britain and France*. Princeton: Princeton University Press, pp. 103–22.
78. Bentham, J. (1952–4), *Jeremy Bentham's Economic Writings*. W. Stark (ed.), 3 vols, London: George Allen and Unwin; and Sigot, N. (2001), *Bentham et l'économie: une histoire d'utilité*. Paris: Economica.

79. Hume, L. J. (1981), *Bentham and Bureaucracy*. Cambridge: Cambridge University Press.
80. For a survey of the debate concerning Bentham's influence in this respect see Conway, S. (1990), 'Bentham and the nineteenth-century revolution in government', in R. Bellamy (ed.), *Victorian Liberalism: Nineteenth-Century Political Thought and Practice*. London: Routledge, pp. 71–80.
81. Bentham, J. (2001), *Writings on the Poor Laws: Vol. I*. M. Quinn (ed.), Oxford: Clarendon Press; and Poynter, J. R. (1969), *Society and Pauperism: English Ideas on Poor Relief, 1795–1834*. London: Routledge & Kegan Paul. See further Chapter 4, pp. 79–90 below.
82. See Bentham, J. (1983b), *Chrestomathia*. M. J. Smith and W. H. Burston (eds), Oxford: Clarendon Press.
83. See Burns, J. H. (1962), *Jeremy Bentham and University College*. London: UCL.
84. British Library Additional Manuscript 33,550, fo 4 (15 October 1814).
85. See pp. 50–3 below.
86. See 'Essay on the influence of time and place on matters of legislation', in Bowring, i. 169–94.

CHAPTER TWO: WHICH BENTHAM?

1. For a more elaborate discussion see Skinner, Q. (2002), *Visions of Politics. Volume I: Regarding Method*. Cambridge: Cambridge University Press, pp. 90–102.
2. See Chapter 6, p. 118 below.
3. See p. 4 above.
4. See p. 14 above.
5. See ibid.
6. On different approaches to the reading of juristic texts see Twining, W. L. (1997), 'Reading law', in *Law in Context: Enlarging a Discipline*. Oxford: Clarendon Press, pp. 198–221. Twining pursues the theme in relation to Bentham in Twining, W. L. (1989), 'Reading Bentham'. *Proceedings of the British Academy*, 85, 97–141.
7. See Lieberman, D. (2000), 'Economy and polity in Bentham's science of legislation', in S. Collini, R. Whatmore and B. Young (eds), *Economy, Polity, and Society: British Intellectual History 1750–1950*. Cambridge: Cambridge University Press, pp. 107–34, at p. 108.
8. See, for instance, Ben Dor, *Constitutional Limits*; Postema, *Bentham and the Common Law Tradition*; Harrison, R. (1983), *Bentham*. London: Routledge & Kegan Paul; and Kelly, *Utilitarianism and Distributive Justice*.
9. Ayer, A. J. (1948), 'The principle of utility', in G. W. Keeton and G. Schwarzenberger (eds), *Jeremy Bentham and the Law*. London: Stevens & Sons, pp. 245–59.
10. See pp. 44–50 below.
11. Ayer, 'Principle of utility', pp. 254–5.

167

12. Bentham, J. (1968), *The Correspondence of Jeremy Bentham: Vol. I.* T. L. S. Sprigge (ed.), London: Athlone, pp. v–viii.
13. See Chapter 8, pp. 153–5 below.
14. Mill, J. S. (1981), *Autobiography and Literary Essays. (The Collected Works of John Stuart Mill: Vol. I.)* J. M. Robson and J. Stillinger (eds), Toronto: University of Toronto Press, pp. 1–290.
15. This became apparent when I assisted Berlin's editor Hugo Hardy in tracking down the sources for Berlin's quotations from Bentham.
16. Bentham, J. (1931), *The Theory of Legislation.* C. K. Ogden (ed.), London: Kegan Paul, Trench, Trubner & Co., p. l.
17. See pp. 94–115 below.
18. See Bowring, ii. 375–487.
19. Bentham, *Rights, Representation, and Reform*, p. 330. For what follows see the Editorial Introduction, pp. xlv–liii.
20. Bentham, J. (1816), *Tactique des assemblées législatives, suivie d'un traité des sophismes politiques.* É. Dumont (ed.), 2 vols, Geneva and Paris: J. J. Paschoud, ii. p. vii.
21. Bowring, x. 497–8.
22. Bentham, J. (1945), *The Limits of Jurisprudence Defined.* C. W. Everett (ed.), New York: Columbia University Press. Everett's title has no textual basis in Bentham's writings.
23. Hart, *Essays on Bentham*, p. 108.
24. For the sanctions see Chapter 3, pp. 48–9 below.
25. Bentham, *Of Laws in General*, p. 16.
26. See UC lxxxviii. 100a.
27. Bentham, *Of Laws in General*, p. 17 n. i.
28. See UC lxxxviii. 100b.
29. See p. 25 and n. 12 above.
30. The volume of writings on the French Revolution also contains 'Supply – New Species Proposed' and 'Short Views of Economy for the use of the French Nation but not unapplicable to the English' which might be considered 'economic writings'.
31. Mill, J. S. (1991), *Indexes to the Collected Works. (The Collected Works of John Stuart Mill: Vol. XXXIII.)* J. O'Grady and J. M. Robson (eds), Toronto: University of Toronto Press.

CHAPTER THREE: THE PRINCIPLE OF UTILITY

1. The former is *Of Laws in General*, soon to be reissued as *Of the Limits of the Penal Branch of Jurisprudence*: see Chapter 2, pp. 39–42 above.
2. *IPML* , p. 11.
3. Ibid., p. 283 n. b.
4. Bentham, '*Legislator of the World*', p. 256.
5. This famous phrase does not appear in *IPML*, but in *A Fragment on Government*, p. 393. After the publication of *A Fragment on Government* in 1776, the phrase does not reappear in Bentham's writings until the 1810s: see Burns, J. H. (2005), 'Happiness and utility: Jeremy Bentham's equation'. *Utilitas*, 17 (1), 46–61.

6. *IPML*, p. 3 n. a.
7. Ibid., p. 13.
8. Ibid., pp. 34–7. For present purposes I have ignored the physical sanction (pleasures and pains which arise from the actions of nature), and Bentham's later 'discovery' of several additional sanctions. For a more complete account see Schofield, *Utility and Democracy*, pp. 35–7.
9. *IPML*, p. 38.
10. Ibid., pp. 38–40.
11. Ibid., p. 11 n. a. This note was written in July 1822.
12. For what follows see Bentham, J. (1997), *De l'ontologie et autres textes sur les fictions*. P. Schofield, J. P. Cléro and C. Laval (eds), Paris: Éditions du Seuil.
13. See pp. 17–18 above.
14. Bentham, *Fragment on Government*, pp. 494–5 n. b.
15. See Chapter 7, pp. 139–40 below.
16. *IPML*, p. 116.
17. Bentham, *First Principles*, pp. 232–4.
18. Bentham, J. (1983c), *Deontology together with A Table of the Springs of Action and Article on Utilitarianism*. A. Goldworth (ed.), Oxford: Clarendon Press, pp. 99–100.
19. See Finnis, J. (1980), *Natural Law and Natural Rights*. Oxford: Clarendon Press, pp. 81–99.
20. See Nozick, R. (1974), *Anarchy, State, and Utopia*. Oxford: Blackwell, pp. 42–5.
21. See Bentham, *Deontology*, pp. 79–86.
22. See p. 129–35 below.
23. See *IPML*, pp. 51–73.
24. See Chapter 5, pp. 104–5 below.
25. Bentham, '*Legislator of the World*', pp. 250–5.
26. Warke, T. (2000b), 'Multi-dimensional utility and the index number problem: Jeremy Bentham, J. S. Mill, and qualitative hedonism'. *Utilitas*, 12 (2), 176–203.
27. Barry, B. (1995), *Justice as Impartiality*. Oxford: Clarendon Press, pp. 145–59.
28. Rawls, J. (1999), *A Theory of Justice* (revised edn) Oxford: Oxford University Press, pp. 19–30.
29. For an excellent discussion of Bentham's opposition to slavery see Rosen, F. (2005), 'Jeremy Bentham on slavery and the slave trade', in B. Schultz and G. Varouxakis (eds), *Utilitarianism and Empire*. Lanham, MD: Lexington Books, pp. 33–56.
30. Rawls, *Theory of Justice*, pp. 65–6.
31. See Bentham, J. (1993), *Official Aptitude Maximized; Expense Minimized*. P. Schofield (ed.), Oxford: Clarendon Press, p. 352.
32. See Chapter 1, p. 7 above.
33. See Chapter 7, pp. 139–40 below.
34. Bentham, J. (1827), *Rationale of Judicial Evidence, specially applied to English practice*. J. S. Mill (ed.), 5 vols, London: Hunt and Clarke, iv. 475 (reprinted in Bowring, vii. 334).

35. Bentham, *Official Aptitude Maximized*, pp. 357–63.
36. For an excellent discussion of this question in relation to John Stuart Mill see Crisp, R. (1997), *Mill on Utilitarianism*. London: Routledge, pp. 135–53.
37. Smart, J. J. C. and Williams, B. (1973), *Utilitarianism for and against*. Cambridge: Cambridge University Press, pp. 149–50.
38. For what follows see Bentham, *'Legislator of the World'*, pp. 194–206.
39. Quinn, M. (2008), 'A failure to reconcile the irreconcilable? Security, subsistence and equality in Bentham's writings on the civil code and on the poor laws'. *History of Political Thought*, 29 (2), 320–43.
40. See 'Manual of Political Economy', in Bentham, *Economic Writings*, i. 219–68.
41. Bentham, *First Principles*, p. 251.
42. Bentham, *Fragment on Government*, pp. 442–8.
43. Kymlicka, W. (2002), *Contemporary Political Philosophy: An Introduction* (2nd edn) Oxford: Oxford University Press, pp. 10–101.
44. *IPML*, pp. 21–33.
45. Ibid., pp. 25–6.

CHAPTER FOUR: PANOPTICON

1. Himmelfarb, G. (1968), *Victorian Minds*. London: Weidenfeld & Nicolson, pp. 32–81; Bahmueller, C. (1981), *The National Charity Company: Jeremy Bentham's Silent Revolution*. Berkeley: University of California Press; and Manning, D. J. (1968), *The Mind of Jeremy Bentham*. Westport, CT: Greenwood.
2. Foucault, *Discipline and Punish*, esp. pp. 195–228.
3. Bowring, iv. 39.
4. See p. 11 above.
5. For a detailed account of Samuel's activities in Russia, and of Jeremy's journey and sojourn there, see Christie, I. R. (1993), *The Benthams in Russia 1780–1791*. Oxford: Berg.
6. Bowring, iv. 40.
7. Ibid., iv. 40–1.
8. Ibid., iv. 45.
9. Ibid., iv. 46–7.
10. Ibid., iv. 47.
11. Ibid., iv. 47–9.
12. Ibid., iv. 49–51.
13. Ibid., iv. 52–3.
14. Ibid., iv. 54.
15. Ibid., iv. 55.
16. Ibid., iv. 62.
17. Beattie, J. M. (1986), *Crime and the Courts in England 1660–1800*. Princeton: Princeton University Press, pp. 301–6.
18. Bowring, iv. 78.
19. Ibid., iv. 67–8.
20. Ibid., iv. 71–2.

21. Ibid., iv. 74.
22. Ibid., iv. 80–1.
23. Ibid., iv. 83–5.
24. Ibid., iv. 81–2 n. ‡.
25. Ibid., iv. 121–2.
26. Ibid., iv. 122–5.
27. Ibid., iv. 125–9.
28. Ibid., iv. 141–2.
29. Ibid., iv. 144.
30. Ibid., iv. 156–63.
31. Ibid., iv. 166–8.
32. Ibid., iv. 168–9.
33. See Bentham, *Writings on the Poor Laws: Vol. I.*
34. Ibid., p. 3.
35. 'Table of cases calling for relief', in ibid., before p. 1.
36. 'Pauper Management Improved', bk I, in Bentham, J. (2009), *Writings on the Poor Laws: Vol. II.* M. Quinn (ed.), Oxford: Clarendon Press.
37. Ibid., bk I, § 6.
38. Ibid., bk II, ch. 3.
39. Ibid., bk II, ch. 4, § 2.
40. Ibid., bk II, ch. 4, § 3.
41. Ibid., bk II, ch. 4, § 4.
42. Ibid., bk II, ch. 4, § 5, and 'Outline of a work entitled Pauper Management Improved', bk II, ch. VI, in ibid.
43. See Malthus, T. R. (1992), *An Essay on the Principle of Population.* D. Winch (ed.), Cambridge: Cambridge University Press, pp. 286–7.
44. See Mill, J. S. (1965), *Principles of Political Economy. (The Collected Works of John Stuart Mill: Vol. III.)* V. W. Bladen and J. M. Robson (eds), Toronto: University of Toronto Press, p. 961.
45. Bentham, *Writings on the Poor Laws: Vol. II,* bk III.
46. See p. 1 above.
47. Bentham, *Writings on the Poor Laws: Vol. II,* bk V, ch. 1.
48. For a detailed account of Bentham's attempt to build the panopticon prison see Semple, *Bentham's Prison,* pp. 166–281.
49. See pp. 9–13 above.
50. See Schofield, *Utility and Democracy,* pp. 250–71.
51. Bentham, *Writings on the Poor Laws: Vol. I,* p. 277.
52. Bentham, J. (1995b), *The Panopticon Writings.* M. Božovič (ed.), London: Verso, pp. 8–11.
53. See pp. 10–11 above.
54. See Bentham, *Constitutional Code: Vol. I,* pp. 438–57.

CHAPTER FIVE: POLITICAL FALLACIES

1. Bentham to Place, late 1820? in Bentham, J. (1994), *The Correspondence of Jeremy Bentham: Vol. X.* S. Conway (ed.), Oxford: Clarendon Press, p. 251.
2. See pp. 35–6 above.

3. See Bingham's 'Preface' reprinted in Bowring, ii. 376.
4. Bowring, ii. 381–2.
5. UC ciii. 1 ([10 June] 1811) [Bowring, ii. 379]. I have based my account on Bentham's original manuscripts, but given the place of the equivalent passage in Bowring for ease of reference.
6. See Browne, T. (1646), *Pseudodoxia Epidemica: or, Enquiries into Very Many Received Tenents, and Commonly Presumed Truths*. London, the running title of which reads '*Enquiries into Vulgar and Common Errors*'.
7. UC ciii. 7–8 (4–5 August 1811) [Bowring, ii. 380]. See further pp. 105–6 below.
8. UC ciii. 10–11 (6–7 August 1811) [Bowring, ii. 380–1].
9. UC ciii. 512–13 (7 February 1811) [Bowring, ii. 474].
10. See Chapter 1, pp. 11–12 above.
11. UC ciii. 517–19 (29 May 1811) [Bowring, ii. 475].
12. UC ciii. 525 (28 June 1810) [Bowring, ii. 476].
13. These were the sentiments which Bentham associated with Blackstone's defence of the British Constitution: see Chapter 1, p. 5 above.
14. UC ciii. 530–2 (28 June 1810) [Bowring, ii. 477].
15. UC ciii. 540 (6 August 1811) [Bowring, ii. 478].
16. Bentham, *First Principles*, p. 151.
17. UC ciii. 535 (29 May 1810) [Bowring, ii. 477].
18. Bentham, *First Principles*, pp. 151, 180–2.
19. UC ciii. 541–3 (28, 30 May 1811) [Bowring, ii. 478–9].
20. Bentham, *First Principles*, pp. 106–7.
21. UC ciii. 45–54 (22–4, 26–8 May 1811) [Bowring, ii. 388–90] and 'Plan of parliamentary reform', in Bowring, iii. 497–8, 500.
22. UC ciii. 64–5 (18 July 1810) [Bowring, ii. 391].
23. UC ciii. 66–7, 69 (17 October 1810) [Bowring, ii. 391–2].
24. Bentham, *First Principles*, pp. 154–5.
25. Ibid., p. 155 n. 1.
26. Ibid., p. 175.
27. 'On the liberty of the press, and public discussion', in Bowring, ii. 277, 279–80.
28. UC ciii. 560–5 (3–4 August 1819) [Bowring, ii. 482–4].
29. *The Guardian*, 2 February 2006, p. 12.
30. See Bentham, *Constitutional Code: Vol. I*, p. 36.
31. Bentham, *First Principles*, pp. 261–3.
32. Ibid., pp. 211–12.
33. UC ciii. 96–7; civ. 152–8 (7, 27 June 1810) [Bowring, ii. 398].
34. UC ciii. 113–14 (20 July 1810) [Bowring, ii. 401].
35. UC ciii. 115; civ. 223 (21 July 1810) [Bowring, ii. 401–2].
36. UC ciii. 123 (24 June 1811) [Bowring, ii. 403].
37. UC ciii. 174; civ. 249 (1, 4 July 1811) [Bowring, ii. 407].
38. UC civ. 385 (1 July 1811).
39. UC ciii. 156 (1 July 1811).
40. UC ciii. 122 (7 July 1811) [Bowring, ii. 402–3].

41. UC ciii. 153 ([?] July 1811). See further Schwartzberg, M. (2007), 'Jeremy Bentham on fallibility and infallibility'. *Journal of the History of Ideas*, 68 (4), 563–85.
42. Judges 11: 30–40.
43. UC civ. 215 (5 July 1810).
44. UC ciii. 160–1 (24 June 1811) [Bowring, ii. 408].
45. UC ciii. 381 (6 July 1810) [Bowring, ii. 448].
46. UC ciii. 217 (27 June 1811) [Bowring, ii. 416].
47. *The Guardian*, 21 November 2005.
48. UC ciii. 289–92 (26 June 1810) [Bowring, ii. 430–1].
49. UC ciii. 309 (10 May 1808).
50. UC ciii. 201 (25 June 1811) [Bowring, ii. 414].
51. *The Guardian*, 24 November 2005.
52. UC ciii. 326–9 (9 July 1810, [?] June 1811) [Bowring, ii. 436–7].
53. Tony Woodley, Joint General Secretary of Unite, press release of 24 September 2007.
54. UC ciii. 578–82 (5 February 1811) [Bowring, ii. 486].
55. See Bentham, J. (2006), *The Correspondence of Jeremy Bentham: Vol. XII*. L. O'Sullivan and C. Fuller (eds), Oxford: Clarendon Press, p. 403 n. 4.
56. UC ciii. 75–6 (24 May 1811) [Bowring, ii. 393].

CHAPTER SIX: RELIGION AND SEX

1. See p. 2 above.
2. See Bentham, *Church-of-Englandism*, Preface, pp. xix–xxi.
3. BL Add. MS 29,809, fos 10–12.
4. [Bentham, J. and Grote, G.] (1822), *Analysis of the Influence of Natural Religion on the Temporal Happiness of Mankind*. London: R. Carlile, p. 3.
5. See p. 20 above.
6. See 'Bentham's last will and testament', pp. 10–11, in Crimmins, J. E. (2002), *Bentham's Auto-Icon and Related Writings*. Bristol: Thoemmes (this book lacks continuous pagination).
7. BL Add. MS 29,807, fo 157.
8. Ibid., fos 151–5.
9. Ibid., fos 158–60.
10. Paley, W. (1802), *Natural Theology: or, Evidences of the Existence and Attributes of the Deity, collected from the Appearances of Nature*. London: A. Faulder.
11. BL Add. MS 29809, fo 20.
12. Ibid., fos 151–3.
13. BL Add. MS 29,807, fos 151–2.
14. BL Add. MS 29,809, fo 169.
15. Singer, P. (1993), *Practical Ethics*. (2nd edn) Cambridge: Cambridge University Press, pp. 55–82.
16. BL Add. MS 29,809, fo 172.

17. BL Add. MS 29,809, fos 49–52.
18. Ibid., fos 257–8.
19. Matthew 7.12.
20. BL Add. MS 29,808, fos 66–8.
21. Ibid., fos 70, 73–4.
22. BL Add. MS 29,808, fo 84.
23. Matthew 6.26, 28, 31, 34.
24. Matthew 5.40–2.
25. Matthew 10.34–6; Luke 12.49–53.
26. BL Add. MS 29,808, fo 94.
27. Ibid., fo 129.
28. Ibid., fos 133–4.
29. Ibid., fo 139. See further pp. 133–4 below.
30. BL Add. MS 29,808, fo 153.
31. BL Add. MS 29,807, fos 44–50.
32. Ibid., fos 58–62.
33. *IPML*, pp. 17–18.
34. BL Add. MS 29,808, fo 4.
35. That Jesus and Mary Magdalene did have children is the conceit of Dan Brown's popular novel *The Da Vinci Code*. Bentham makes Brown's thesis appear very tame indeed!
36. The allusion is to Leviticus 20.13, 15.
37. Blackstone, *Commentaries on the Laws of England*, iv. 216.
38. Leviticus 20.18.
39. Leviticus 19.19.
40. Leviticus 21.9.
41. Deuteronomy 22.22.
42. Leviticus 20.9.
43. BL Add. MS 29,808, fos 18–20.
44. McNeill, J. J. (1993), *The Church and the Homosexual*. (4th edn) Boston: Beacon, pp. 42–50.
45. Ibid., pp. 56–9.
46. Ibid., p. 147.
47. Mark 14.51–2. There are only 30 verses in Mark which are independent of the two other Synoptic Gospels – Matthew and Luke. Peake's *Commentary*, published 1919, on Mark (written by H. G. Wood) refers to this as 'A curious little incident peculiar to Mark', and suggests that it might be 'interpreted as a personal experience of the evangelist, as his signature to his portrait of Jesus'.
48. Crompton, L. (1985), *Bryon and Greek Love: Homophobia in 19th-Century England*. London; Faber & Faber, pp. 280–3, notes that Bentham had seen a reference to this incident, which suggested the youth was a male prostitute, in the *Monthly Magazine* of 1811.
49. BL Add. MS 29,808, fos 6–11.
50. John 13.23.
51. John 13.25.
52. Most modern commentators allow that the *Song of Solomon*, an anthology of love poems, was intended as an erotic work, though Christian

tradition generally interpreted it as an allegory of God's relationship with the Church or the soul.
53. BL Add. MS 29,808, fos 13–17.
54. UC clx. 1–2; lxx. 25; lxix. 139.
55. BL Add. MS 29,808, fo 134.

CHAPTER SEVEN: TORTURE

1. See [2005] UKHL 71.
2. See pp. 67–9 above.
3. Bentham, *First Principles*, pp. 184–5.
4. Bentham, *'Legislator of the World'*, pp. 123–5.
5. Ibid., para 12.
6. See Gatrell, V. A. C. (1994), *The Hanging Tree: Execution and the English People*. Oxford: Oxford University Press, p. 617.
7. 'Truth versus Ashhurst; or, law as it is, contrasted with what it is said to be', in Bowring, v. 232–3.
8. [2005] UKHL 71, para. 81.
9. See, for instance, Blackstone, *Commentaries on the Laws of England*, i. 69–70.
10. 'Truth versus Ashhurst', in Bowring, v. 235.
11. [2005] UKHL 71, para. 82.
12. See p. 9 above.
13. Bentham, *Rights, Representation, and Reform*, p. 317.
14. Ibid., p. 330.
15. Bentham, *Securities against Misrule*, pp. 23–4 n. a.
16. Bentham, *Rights, Representation, and Reform*, pp. 263–88. See also Chapter 5, pp. 105–8 above.
17. Bentham, *Rights, Representation, and Reform*, pp. 405–18.
18. Schofield, *Utility and Democracy*, pp. 225–37.
19. *IPML*, p. 11.
20. [2005] UKHL 71, para. 51.
21. Twining, *Bentham and Wigmore on Evidence*, p. 42.
22. Ibid., p. 70.
23. [2005] UKHL 71, para. 13.
24. Bowring, vii. 454.
25. Bentham, *Constitutional Code: Vol. I*, pp. 173–86.
26. 'Constitutional Code', ch. XXXIII, § VI, art 17, at Bowring, ix. 595.
27. 'Letters to Count Toreno', in Bowring, viii. 501.
28. UC lxix. 180–6 (14–15 August 1804).
29. UC civ. 101 (20 July 1810).
30. UC lxix. 162–74 (13 August 1804).
31. Twining, W. L. and Twining, P. E. (1973), 'Bentham on Torture', in M. H. James (ed.), *Bentham and Legal Theory*, pp. 39–90, at p. 43 (reprinted from *Northern Ireland Legal Quarterly*, 24 (3)).
32. Ibid., p. 64.
33. Ibid., p. 67.
34. Ibid., pp. 47–8, 71.

35. Ibid., pp. 50–2, 66.
36. Ibid., pp. 52–3.
37. [2005] UKHL 71, para. 26.
38. Twining and Twining, 'Bentham on Torture', p. 59.
39. Ibid., p. 60.
40. Ibid., pp. 52–4.
41. Berlin, I. (1997), *The Proper Study of Mankind: An Anthology of Essays.* H. Hardy and H. Hausheer (eds), London: Chatto & Windus, p. 194. See further Rosen, F. (1990), *Thinking about Liberty.* London: University College London.
42. Bentham, *Of Laws in General*, pp. 119–20, 253–4.
43. Bentham, *Rights, Representation, and Reform*, p. 339.
44. Bentham, *'Legislator of the World'*, p. 140 n. b.
45. See Hobbes, T. (1991), *Leviathan.* R. Tuck (ed.), Cambridge: Cambridge University Press, pp. 88–90.
46. See Bentham to Reginald Pole Carew, 20 April 1804, in Bentham, *Correspondence: Vol. VII*, pp. 264–6.
47. Bowring, i. 557.
48. See 'Bentham's last will and testament', in Crimmins, *Bentham's Auto-Icon.*
49. The wax head was made by the French anatomical modeller Jacques Talrich: see Fuller, *The Old Radical*, pp. 51–2.
50. Only twenty or thirty copies of the pamphlet were run off, and of these only three are known to survive.
51. 'Auto-Icon; or, farther uses of the dead to the living', p. 3, in Crimmins, *Bentham's Auto-Icon.*
52. Ibid., p. 15.
53. Ibid., pp. 9–10.

INDEX

Oxford, University of 3, 4, 17, 116
see also Queen's College, Oxford

pain and pleasure 4, 6–7, 18, 44–50,
53–60, 120, 122, 124, 125, 145
Paley, William 119–20
Palladio, Andrea 123–4
pannomion 7–8
panopticon prison 10, 11–12, 16,
18, 70–9, 90–3, 151
see also industry-house
panopticon
paraphrasis 52–3
parliamentary reform 10, 12–13,
36, 93, 94–5
Paul the Apostle 117–18, 130,
131–2
peace 16–17, 126
penal code 4, 8, 13, 44, 50, 71, 148
perception 51, 136
person, security for 7, 9, 63,
139, 150
personal identity 121–4, 151
Peter, disciple of Jesus 133
Petty, William, 2nd Earl of
Shelburne and 1st Marquis
of Lansdowne 14
Phillips, Nicholas, Baron Phillips
of Worth Matravers 109
phraseoplerosis 52
pilgrimage 152
Pitt the Younger, William 80,
107–8
Place, Francis 95, 117, 118
Plato 19
pleasure *see* pain and pleasure
police 48, 108–11, 132, 133
Ponceau, Peter de 139
poor law 10, 17, 79–90
population 66, 89
Portugal 13
Potemkin, Prince Grigoriy
Aleksandrovich 11, 72

poverty 80–1
power 5, 8, 46, 70, 120
see also administrative power;
executive power; separation
of powers
preference satisfaction 24, 60
prejudice 98–101
Prescott, John 112
press, liberty of 102
Priestley, Joseph 4, 14
priests 144, 145
primogeniture 111
probity 99
promise-keeping 67
property 7, 9, 63, 65–6, 126,
139, 150
prostitution 110–11, 130, 132–3
psychology 23–4, 44–50, 53–60
public opinion (tribunal) 48, 73,
84, 93
punishment and reward 6–7, 8,
16, 48–50, 53, 71, 77, 92, 117,
120, 129, 146

Queen's College, Oxford 2
Queen's Square Place,
Westminster 3

radicalism, political 4, 9–13, 50,
63, 93
Raphael 124
Rawls, John 61–3, 67, 68–9
real and fictitious entities 17–18,
51–3
recycling 82–3
religion 2, 7, 15, 50, 116–36, 152
remuneratory code 8
representative democracy 10,
16, 94
republicanism 13, 16, 18, 91, 93
reputation 7, 9, 63, 65, 103, 139, 150
Reveley, Willey 74, 75
reward *see* punishment and reward

Richardson, Samuel 2
right and wrong 4, 68–9, 144–5
    see also ethics; morality
rights, declarations of 37–9, 106,
    108, 137–8, 139–40, 151
rights and duties 8, 53, 63, 139
    see also silence, right to
Robbins, Lionel 21
Romanticism 18
Romilly, Samuel 14
Rose, Michael 112
rule utilitarianism 67
rulers 11–12, 102–3, 104, 108
rules 8–9, 65, 67, 135
Russia 11, 71–2

St James's Park 3
St Petersburg 21
Salas, Ramón de 14
sanctions 8, 40, 48–50
    see also punishment and
    reward
security 7, 8, 9, 63, 65–7, 135, 139,
    140, 149–51
self-regard 54–5, 102–3
Senior, Nassau 90
separation of powers 140–1
Sermon on the Mount 125–7
sex 7, 50, 125, 129–35
Shelburne *see* Petty
Sieyès, Emmanuel 37
silence, right to 148
Simon, Siôn 112
sinecures 63
Singer, Peter 123
single seatedness 143
sinister interests 11–12, 35–6, 48,
    91, 93, 97–105
Smart, J. J. C. 64
Smith, Adam 65
Smith, Richard 38
Smith, Thomas Southwood 152
Smyrna 72

social contract 5, 108
Sodom and Gomorrah 130–1
sovereignty 5–6, 7, 40–1
Spain 13, 14, 33–4, 41–2
Spanish America 13, 22
Srebenica 112
Star Chamber 138
status *see* condition in life
Sterne, Laurence 2
subsistence 8, 63, 65–7, 81, 89
substantive law 8
suffering 4, 45
suffrage 10, 12, 16, 93
suicide 121, 124–5, 136
surveillance *see* inspection
Swift, Jonathan 1–2
sympathy 54–5, 68–9

Talleyrand-Périgord, Charles
    Maurice de 14
tattoos 151
taxation 66, 111
terrorism 98, 108–10, 137, 148
textual editing 19–43
torture 137–49
Townsend, Joseph 80
trade 66
transportation 71, 91
Traynor, Ian 112
Tripoli 13
truth 19, 96, 100, 101, 102,
    114–15, 142
Twining, William 141–2

understanding 46
United States of America 5–6, 13,
    18, 99, 102, 104
University College London 17, 21,
    30, 118, 152
utilitarianism *see* utility,
    principle of
utility, principle of 4, 16, 18, 23–4,
    44–69, 97, 114–15, 150